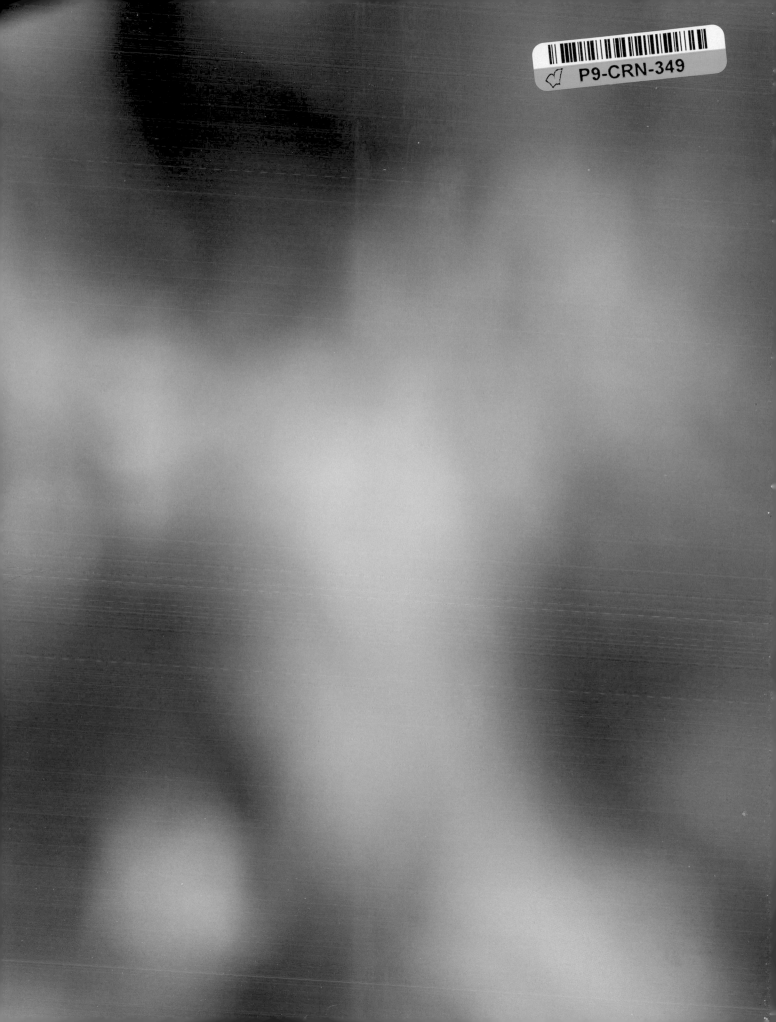

Haynes

Garden
Wildlife
Manual

First published in April 2015

A catalogue record for this book is available from the
British Library

ISBN 978 0 85733 307 0

Published by Haynes Publishing,
Sparkford, Yeovil, Somerset BA22 7JJ, UK
Tel: 01963 442030 Fax: 01963 440001
Int. tel: +44 1963 442030 Int. fax: +44 1963 440001
E-mail: sales@haynes.co.uk
Website: www.haynes.co.uk

Haynes North America Inc.
861 Lawrence Drive, Newbury Park,
California 91320, USA

Printed in the USA by Odcombe Press LP,
1299 Bridgestone Parkway, La Vergne, TN 37086

Credits

Author:	Gerard Cheshire
Project Manager:	Louise McIntyre
Copy editor:	Ian Heath
Page designer:	James Robertson
Illustrator:	Ian Moores

Haynes

Garden Wildlife
Manual

The complete guide
to attracting wildlife
into your garden

Gerard Cheshire

CONTENTS

Amphibians and reptiles

Invertebrates

Plants and fungi

FOREWORD

Gardens and urban parks are not only great places to unwind and take pleasure from nature, they are becoming increasingly important havens for wildlife. Let Gerard Cheshire be your guide to the surprisingly large array of animals and plants that can be found in Britain's gardens. Knowing what you're looking at makes the experience more enjoyable and, if you're not already, will shift you from being a passive observer of the natural world to someone who values and wants to conserve it.

As you'd expect from a Haynes Manual, this is more than an illustrated reference to what you might see, it's a practical guide to making your garden a better place for wildlife. From advice on what to plant to encourage butterflies to DIY bird tables that allow robins in, but keep pigeons out, the emphasis is on the simple and sustainable. Nest boxes can be constructed from a single plank of wood that you might find in a skip. You can turn the discarded plastic packaging from a toy car into an observable ant colony. This book provides practical advice on how to encourage nature, observe nature and get more from your garden and its inhabitants.

In the academic world, 'restoration ecology' is the rather grand title given to the growing field of research on how environments that have been damaged by humans can be restored to normal healthy function. You can play your own important part here. It starts with your own garden or back yard, but you can go further: get your local school involved with 'eco' projects, scrutinise planning permission notices for felling trees and concreting over front gardens, and make sure your council lives up to the 'green' promises in its publicity leaflets.

Preserving 'the countryside' is important, but it is important to realise that urban environments are not lost to nature. With a little help from us, gardens become not only wildlife havens in their own right, but vital corridors between larger green spaces such as parks and suburban woodlands. Whether you can already tell the difference between a chiffchaff and a willow warbler at 50 paces, or struggle to differentiate a starling from a blackbird, Gerard Cheshire's book will give you inspiration to get outdoors and do some 'restoration ecology' in your own garden. The natural world is on your doorstep; enjoy it, help it.

Innes Cuthill,
Professor of Behavioural Ecology,
University of Bristol

INTRODUCTION

When we consider all of the species of wildlife that can be found in our gardens, we might wonder how they are arranged in scientific terms. In truth, arguments still continue about the best way to classify life forms, because it depends on the way this is done. Traditional taxonomy is based on shared characteristics, but this can be misleading when unrelated species happen to be similar. Modern cladistics is based on shared evolution, but this can lead to unfamiliar ways of dividing up species. For the sake of simplicity, this book classifies species into two broad kingdoms, which are not strictly scientific but are commonly used and understood. These are fauna (vertebrate animals and invertebrate animals) and flora (plants and fungi).

Vertebrate animals include mammals, birds, reptiles, amphibians and fish. Though fish are an important part of the ecosystem as a whole, they have been excluded from this book because very few people are lucky enough to have gardens able to accommodate wild British species – ie with lakes, streams, rivers, an estuary or a stretch of coastline. Marine life is not included for similar reasons.

Invertebrate animals include all of the species lower down the evolutionary scale. Instead of having bones, they either have exoskeletons or soft bodies. Those with exoskeletons include insects, crustaceans, arachnids, millipedes and centipedes. Those with soft bodies include molluscs and worms.

Plants come in two basic types. There are flowering plants, which produce seeds, and there are non-flowering plants, which produce spores. Flowering plants include grasses, flowers, herbs, climbers, shrubs and trees. Non-flowering plants include ferns, mosses, liverworts and algae. Fungi also produce spores and include toadstools, mushrooms, moulds and mildews. There are also lichens, which are algae and fungi living in union. This is known as a symbiotic relationship and means that the organisms bring benefits to each other. Mosses and lichens are able to colonise the most unlikely places, such as the surfaces of stone, bricks and roof tiles.

All gardens – whether they are roof terraces, balconies, back yards, urban patches, suburban plots or rural parcels – will contain their own fauna and flora. Animals and plants are very good at finding ways to survive, by colonising habitats wherever they show promise. In fact, it is often the less obvious places that contain communities of unusual species, because these have evolved to make the most of resources where they can live without competition from other species.

If we regard our different gardens as habitats that mimic wild environments then it becomes obvious that we can expect to see particular species establishing themselves in particular corners. This is because they offer different econiches (ecological niches) to be exploited. Some gardens may offer many econiches, while other gardens may offer just one or two. But it doesn't matter to the wildlife, because all of our gardens add up to a vast harlequin patchwork of econiches, microhabitats, habitats and environments. It is all a matter of scale.

Somewhat ironically, our conurbations can offer a wider range of places for wildlife to inhabit than the original landscape. Consequently, they can be home to species that would otherwise not exist in those areas. Of course, there are also some species that do not thrive alongside our town and city sprawl, which is why it is necessary to establish conservation sites in appropriate locations around the country.

The average British garden covers an area of about one fiftieth (0.02) of an acre, which is equal to around 900ft^2: ie 30 x 30ft or 20 x 45ft. With some 23-million-odd British gardens this comes to a total of approximately half a million acres. This equates to roughly 1% of the habitat available to wildlife in Britain. Although this may not seem much, it is worth remembering that a great deal of Britain is covered by agricultural land that has relatively little value to wildlife, because it is covered by grazing, by arable crops, by plantations and so on; known collectively as monoculture. So, in real terms our gardens account for a far higher percentage of potentially usable habitat: perhaps 10% nationally and much higher in urban areas, where most of the land is given over to tarmac, asphalt, paving and buildings. The operative word here is *potential*, as the focus of this book is on ways to improve our gardens to increase that potential. In order to do this, it is first necessary to

▲ A butterfly on the 'butterfly bush'.

consider the key areas in which our gardens can provide resources for wildlife.

Of course, the many species involved require a vast range of specific resources, but there are some fundamental considerations to be made, which will generally benefit them all and increase the biodiversity (the number of different species) and the fecundity (the number of specimens). All organisms need habitats that provide somewhere to live, somewhere to reproduce and somewhere to find nutrition. These are the basic requirements that will attract wildlife into any habitat, whether they are animals, plants or fungi.

So, the first rule is to imitate nature, by allowing your garden to become less tidy, unkempt, overgrown, *au naturel*. Just by letting things go a bit, you'll find that nature tends to

▼ A '5-star' insect hotel.

take care of itself. This is a process known by ecologists as succession. Wild plants will have a chance to grow, because they are no longer labelled *weeds*. In turn, invertebrates will move in and colonise the patch of wilderness. Then will come the amphibians, reptiles, birds and mammals, all wanting a piece of the action. Before you know it, you'll have a veritable jungle at the end of your garden, filled with all manner of organisms forming their own ecosystem. This ecosystem will also change over time, because succession relies on dynamic change. Ruderal or primary plant species will be replaced by secondary species that, in due course, will be replaced by tertiary species, as the ecosystem matures.

The second rule, therefore, is to introduce a pattern of rotation to your wilderness, so that there is always a patch at a different stage of succession. That way, you'll optimise the number of species living in your garden at any given time. Again, this imitates nature, because wild habitats naturally become patchworks of succession due to the way trees fall to make clearings, or forest and heath fires raze vegetation to the ground and so on, ready for the process of succession to begin again.

The third rule is to imitate habitat transition. In wild habitats there are natural transitions in habitat where grassland meets woodland, with strips of hedgerow where dense undergrowth results. Also, there are occasional changes to the substrate, where less fertile ground, drier ground or waterlogged ground results in a patch with a different ecological signature. Of course, there is also the transition from terrestrial to aquatic habitat, where ponds and lakes are formed. This is known as riparian habitat.

The fourth rule is to imitate habitat inclusions. These are those scattered features in the landscape that create microhabitats, such as rotten stumps, lying logs, rocks, holes, and pools. They provide singular places for certain species to reside, hide, shelter, feed, bask, hibernate and so on. The arbitrary nature of genuine wilderness lends itself to a quite random habitat structure, in which wildlife has evolved to thrive, because it lends itself to increased opportunity with regard to resources.

The fifth rule is to imitate the utilities provided by natural habitats. The cavities in tree trunks and crevices behind bark, which animals use to nest, roost and hibernate, only occur abundantly in mature woodland. Similarly, cliffs and banks with suitable recesses, fissures and clefts are not found in most gardens. So it is necessary to introduce artificial facilities to mimic the hollows, holes and hideouts needed. This is achieved by constructing a variety of boxes, shelters, dens and lairs, each designed to suit a particular purpose and situated in its appropriate location around the garden.

The sixth rule is to supplement the food resources of certain species. This can be done by leaving food out, of course, which is useful for animal watching, but the best way is to encourage the food to grow naturally in your garden. Seeding and planting appropriate herbage will attract invertebrates to feed, either as adults or larvae. Also, those plants will produce their own seeds and fruits. In this way, a foundation is laid for a food web or chain, so that all of the species in the ecosystem can find what they need. Ponds are useful too, as they establish ecosystems that attract invertebrates with aquatic and semi-aquatic life cycles. In addition, their edges provide moist econiches for invertebrates that need to avoid drying out, and they provide freshwater for larger animals to drink. Similarly, deadwood has its own ecosystem based on the fauna and flora of decomposition or decay, which provides food for animals and nutrition for plants. So there are some clear ways of provisioning wildlife with what it needs to establish a healthy ecosystem.

The seventh rule, which many gardeners will dislike, is the banishment of foreign plant species in favour of natives. The same goes for cultivars of native species. There are many such plants in British gardens because they have showy foliage and fancy blooms, but they have no place in the British ecosystem. In that regard, they take up useful space that would be better used to grow plants that are part of the natural landscape and which our native animals have evolved alongside. This strategy may be limiting in terms of variety of hues and texture to the avid gardener, but it makes far more sense to the avid naturalist. So, if your garden is an immaculate palette of colours and shades then it is probably an ecodesert to British wildlife. Beauty is in the eye of the beholder, so try to make your garden look more like a forest glade instead, and the eye of Mother Nature will notice. In short, do the opposite to the general advice given by most so-called *gardeners*, and you'll be along the right tracks.

That doesn't mean that you can't have a garden that isn't well designed and considered, but the aim is to find beauty in nature's imperfection, which is the quality that we all appreciate but cannot definitively explain when we go for a country stroll. It is a primal instinct, because we too come from the wilderness where order, uniformity and tidiness are not matters of administration but occasional accidents that occur in the natural scheme of things. The result is a delicate balance between the random and the organised.

An additional consideration is the movement and migration of wildlife. Many animals can fly or climb trees, fences and walls to travel from one garden to another. However, it is always a good idea to make life easier for some species by leaving ground-level openings. If animals find it easy to move about then they are more likely to enter your garden and stay around. This is especially true of animals that need to roam in search of sufficient food, by treating several gardens as one territory. If you make it inconvenient to visit your garden then they won't bother, because it is a matter of weighing up the possible benefits against the cost in time and energy, and the risk of injury or predation. It pays to understand how animals view their world, as survival and reproduction always constitute the prime directive for all forms of wildlife.

Finally, it is useful to bear in mind that the British garden ordinarily mimics a certain type of natural habitat. This is known generally as mixed woodland and meadow, or forest and grassland, which is typical of Britain and north-western Europe. This means that we can expect a certain roll call of fauna and flora species that are part of that type of ecosystem. It also means that we should not expect other species that belong to other ecosystems, although they may turn up from time to time as vagrants, especially in places where our gardens happen to be near to less typical habitats.

This book therefore covers species that comprise the typical British ecosystem, simply because a wide range of gardens over the whole of Britain needs to be included. In this context the term *typical* is taken to mean those species that are likely to be seen in a reasonable percentage of gardens across Britain, allowing for geographical and seasonal range variations. Inevitably, this means that all gardens will have certain species and not others. Also, once in a while they will have anomalous species that are not included in the book, as well as the occasional rarity passing through.

There is something to be said about the status of British

▼ A privet hawk moth sits quietly on this girl's hand.

species too. Whether species are regarded as common, uncommon, scarce or rare is largely a matter of judgement based on national data that, in turn, relies on information provided by people around the country. The result is that these terms tend to be paired with qualifiers, such as *locally* common, *increasingly* uncommon, *becoming* scarce and *now* rare. Of course, it is quite possible never to have seen a species that is considered common, or to frequently see a species that is considered rare. The truth is that the measure of abundance of different species is largely a relative matter, with so many variables involved that it is not particularly useful to think of species in this way. Britain is, in effect, one giant ecosystem, so the fauna and flora it comprises are always in flux, with considerable fluctuations occurring on a yearly basis. Those fluctuations may be due to natural phenomena, man-made phenomena or a combination of the two.

Historically, the growing human population has resulted in the depletion of British natural habitats over thousands of years. Although some species have taken advantage of the environmental changes and thrived alongside humanity, most species have reduced in overall numbers simply because there are fewer places for them to live. This is where the natural design of our gardens can make a significant difference, by providing more places for our wildlife to set up home. When there are many scattered pockets of habitat in an area it means that species can establish scattered populations, called metapopulations (populations of sub-populations). Although scattered, the sub-populations find

ways to interact with one another. This ensures healthy gene flow and it means that species are better poised to invade new pockets of habitat as and when they appear.

ncidentally, this highlights the importance of *green corridors* – so called because they provide routes of passage for species between pockets of habitat in areas that are otherwise barren of wildlife due to urbanisation. In addition to gardens themselves, green corridors include parks, commons, playgrounds, wasteland, sports grounds, golf courses, school fields, churchyards, hedgerows, tree avenues, railway embankments, verges, rivers and canals. There are few urban places truly devoid of greenery in one form or another, but roads can present real obstacles because of their linear nature. For this reason, wildlife bridges and tunnels are sometimes integrated to allow species the freedom to cross by day or night.

It becomes apparent, then, that wildlife depends on this grid of green corridors and habitats to maintain viable populations across the urban environment. What is more, the *green grid* can account for a surprisingly high percentage of the overall urban surface area. Also, the percentage increases moving farther away from the centre of each town or city. As all species have evolved to survive and reproduce if at all possible, then they always make a go of it no matter what life throws at them. Some do rather better than others in urban environments, but there will always be a considerable diversity of species exploiting what's on offer. If we offer more, by naturally designing our gardens, then it follows that a greater diversity of species will benefit, and that is what this book is all about.

▼ A butterfly finds somewhere unusual to sunbathe!

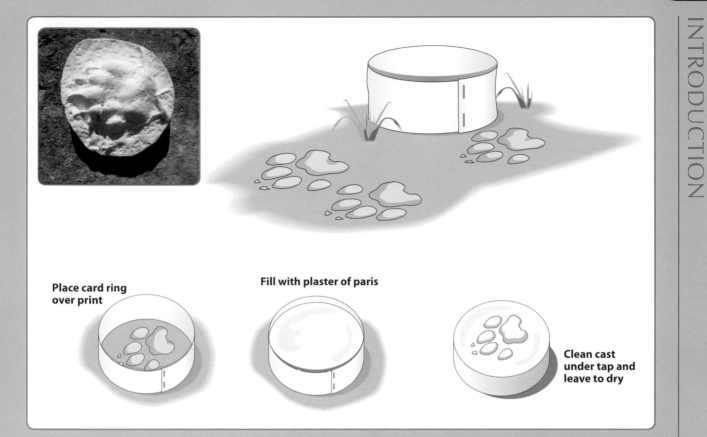

Place card ring over print

Fill with plaster of paris

Clean cast under tap and leave to dry

Nature museum

Whilst it is not ethical to catch and kill animals for a collection, and is in many cases illegal, it is perfectly acceptable to gather random finds to create a nature museum. All sorts of things – including bones, feathers, fossils, pellets, footprint casts, insect cases, reptile skins, egg shells, seashells and pressed flowers – can be displayed as part of your own exhibition. In fact, the more varied the curiosities the better, as that is what makes a museum more interesting, both to you and to anyone else who cares to take a look.

Generally speaking it is more convenient to keep dry and desiccated exhibits, as they are less inclined to denature and emit unpleasant odours of decay. It is also possible to use drying agents and antimicrobial compounds in display cases, to preserve things that might otherwise be inclined to decompose. In addition, certain items may be kept in sealed jars, immersed in preservative fluids such as alcohol, white vinegar or formaldehyde solution.

A tip for making your own museum is to always keep a bag or container on your person when going for walks, wherever you may be – in woods, on beaches, in fields, at the park or in your garden. That way, you can easily collect potential exhibits and keep them intact until you return to your museum. And, as curator, you get to decide what exhibits are on display. Don't forget to label your exhibits too, so that others know what the item is, where it was found and when it was found.

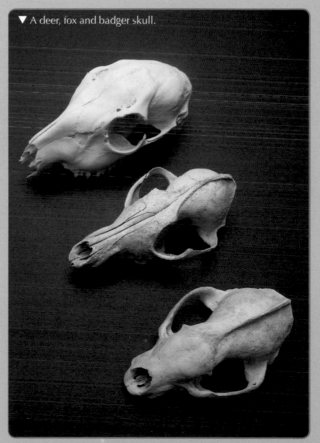

▼ A deer, fox and badger skull.

Project guidelines

The projects in this book have been carefully designed with simplicity of construction in mind. For example, every cut is perpendicular or right-angled, because a 90° cut is easiest to make. The idea is that anyone with a modicum of skill and a basic set of tools should be able to build the projects quite easily by using inexpensive or recycled materials. This means that more people are likely to give them a go, safe in the knowledge that they have the ability, the facilities and the time. Therefore, more wildlife will benefit from their efforts.

Although the examples made and photographed for the book are fairly neat and tidy in appearance, there is no requirement for you to aim for the same appearance and uniformity. As long as they hold together then the wildlife will be perfectly happy with them, so don't worry about the details. You can improvise with whatever tools and materials you have at hand. Also, you might prefer to paint your projects to personalise them, or change their design slightly as you see fit – there are no rules, only guidelines.

In the wild, animals make the most of the varied resources around them and would never find two identical cavities in nature for hibernating, nesting or sheltering. So it is far more important to provide them with your best efforts rather than not bother at all, for fear of embarrassment. The animals will not mind one little bit if your projects are crooked, wonky, quirky, eccentric or charming to the eye, as long as they can use them to go about the business of survival and reproduction. Just go ahead and make your garden a habitat with all manner of holes, homes and hideouts for them to use.

Many of the dimensions are given as multiples of the width (W) and the thickness (T) of a plank of wood. This means that any available plank can be used. It may be a reclaimed floorboard, a leftover plank, a newly purchased piece of timber or something salvaged from a skip – it doesn't matter as long as the wood is solid, flat and straight. Some of the projects require the use of a hole-cutter and a drill, which require appropriate safety precautions, but then it is only a matter of cutting the list of pieces and fixing them together, with either nails or screws. After that, the project needs waterproofing with damp-proof course (DPC) or asphalt as a roof. The wood can also be preserved or painted before the finished project is positioned in the garden.

Most of the projects should take no more than an hour or two to complete, although they may take a while longer if they are adapted and decorated. A few projects are slightly more time-consuming to build because they are larger and have more components, but they are no more difficult to make as they are designed with the same principles in mind. It is worth mentioning that the time taken to execute these projects can be reduced if they are made in batches, because mass production of components and line assembly will increase efficiency. This is known as time-motion planning. If you have a large enough garden, then this may be a worthwhile approach. Similarly, you may wish to make a number of projects as gifts for friends and family. Of course, a parent or teacher may wish to pre-prepare several sets of components to keep a number of children occupied for a few hours.

Project tool list

Hand saw
Hammer
Workbench
G-clamps
Electric drill
Electric and hand screwdrivers
Set-square
Pencil
Craft knife
Tape measure and steel rule
Set of drill-bits
Set of spade-bits
Hand plane
Rasp
Metal file
Set of hole-cutters
Safety glasses
20–50mm screws
40–50mm lost-head nails
20–25mm felt/clout nails
Sandpaper
330mm DPC or roofing felt/asphalt
Scissors
Wood preserver or paint
Paintbrush
40mm hinges (optional)
Fixing bolts
Build timber
Timber offcuts

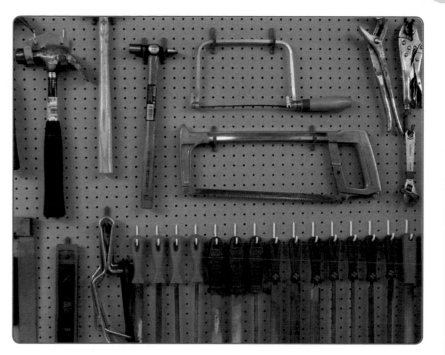

Generic instruction

By following the cutting list you should be able to cut the necessary components for your project, according to the multiples of plank width and plank thickness provided. This means that any plank or board of roughly the right dimensions will do the job.

To assemble the project, simply compare the exploded diagram with the completed diagram to see how the components fit together. You may find that you need to tweak things here and there, depending on how straight and square the pieces are, so it is a good idea to hold things in place before properly fixing them. Once you are sure things are correct then go ahead and assemble.

For projects that have additional battens and dowels, slight alterations to the design may be necessary according to the dimensions of the materials available to you. As long as they are similar to those shown then this should be straightforward enough with the application of a little common sense.

Remember that the point of these projects is to make use of recycled, discarded or leftover pieces of wood, so any fiddling about and adjusting of measurements will be worth the inconvenience. The more projects started and finished the better, as it means plenty of places for garden animals to shelter, to breed and to hibernate.

Where additional materials and fittings are required then by all means use what you have available – as long as they do the job, there is no reason to go and buy extra materials and parts. It may be possible to cannibalise them from other goods that are broken, obsolete or no longer useful. If you do need to purchase bits and pieces then do your best to find things online, as by missing out the middle man these are usually far less expensive. There are also websites dedicated to recycling items, either by auction or by giving things away. Similarly, you might find what you need in builders' skips, at local municipal dumps or at reclamation yards.

Project tips

1   Measure things twice before cutting – it's an old but wise adage.
2   Always secure things safely and wear safety goggles when cutting, drilling or machining.
3   Clamp components against some scrap wood when drilling or hole cutting.
4   Protect your components with scraps to avoid clamp marks.
5   To avoid splitting, use a pilot drill before screwing or nailing.
6   Sand down any rough edges to finish the components neatly.
7   Never rush things, as that is how accidents happen.
8   If necessary, ask a competent adult for help when making the projects and fixing them in place.
9   If you mess something up then put it down to experience and try again – we only learn by making mistakes.
10 Don't ever think you can't do it – think of the satisfaction when you succeed!

MAMMALS

The wild mammals of Britain include cervids (deer), rodents (rats, mice, voles, squirrels, dormice), mustelids (weasels, stoats, martens, badgers), canids (foxes), felids (wild cats), erinacids (hedgehogs), lagomorphs (rabbits, hares), soricids (shrews) and chiroptids (bats). Despite our islands being overcrowded with humanity and their pets, there is still a surprising variety and abundance of wild mammals. We have lost a few species along the way, such as wolves, bear, boar and beaver, but we have gained a few too, such as mink, various deer, coypu, grey squirrels and edible dormice. Actually, even the house mouse and black and brown rats were introduced to our shores from foreign parts.

Mammals give birth to live young, which are then fed on milk. They also have hair, or fur, to insulate their bodies from heat loss, as they are warm-blooded. In Britain, mammals range in size from the impressive red deer down to the diminutive pygmy shrew. In terms of diet, British wild mammals fall into various groups: carnivores eat the flesh of other animals, insectivores eat insects and other invertebrates, herbivores eat plant matter, and omnivores have a catholic, or mixed, diet of both animals and plants. Some mammal species remain active during the winter months, so they need to continue feeding in order to top-up their energy levels. Other species hibernate, in order to save energy by being inactive.

Arboreal rodents

Rodents have evolved to exploit the various econiches available in the natural habitat of the British countryside. Gardens correspond with the woodland, hedge margin and meadow found naturally in Britain, so the species adapted to those environments are now found in our gardens. Voles are terrestrial, while mice and rats are semi-arboreal, but the truly arboreal rodents are dormice and squirrels.

There are two species of dormouse: the hazel dormouse and the edible dormouse. There are also two species of squirrel: the red squirrel and the grey squirrel. The hazel dormouse and the red squirrel are both indigenous species, while the edible dormouse and the grey squirrel are introduced species.

The edible dormouse has its name because it was an ancient Roman delicacy; but it was not introduced to Britain by the Romans. In fact, it escaped from a zoological collection at the turn of the 20th century and has now established a healthy population in the English midlands. As it is really an animal of warmer climates, the edible dormouse prefers to make its home in roof spaces. The grey squirrel arrived under similar circumstances and at a similar time to the edible dormouse, but it originated from a climate in North America much like our own, so it rapidly spread over much of Britain.

Both native species have suffered marked population declines, but they can still be found in gardens in the right places. In the case of the hazel dormouse, its decline is due to the loss of suitable habitat resulting from changes in the use of the British countryside. Hazel coppicing is no longer widely practised, because people seldom use hurdle fencing or wicker baskets, so the hazel dormouse simply has fewer places to make its home. In the case of the red squirrel, it has been replaced by the grey squirrel in areas of deciduous woodland because it is out-competed, largely due to the greater size and territorial aggression of the American species. However, in areas of conifer forest the red squirrel out-competes the grey squirrel, because it is better adapted to feeding from fir cones, so it manages to maintain healthy local and regional populations.

Squirrels are noted for their habit of burying surplus food resources in the autumn months as a larder for the winter months, when food is hard to find. This is an example of a phenomenon known as 'extended phenotype', which is another way of saying that the behaviour benefits the species as a whole, because other individuals may find the

◄ The edible dormouse (*Glis glis*) has become locally common in Britain. The animals nest in the roofs of houses and use gardens as their habitat for foraging. They can be heard clambering about at night through the ceiling.

▼ Although the hazel dormouse (*Muscardis avellanarius*) is suffering from loss of habitat, it probably benefitted from habitat gain in the first place, when the British once managed vast areas of hazel coppice for a plethora of traditional uses.

◄ The grey squirrel (*Sciurus carolinensis*) has become a familiar sight across Britain, where it is loved and loathed in equal measure. It owes much of its success to its boldness of character, which enables it to acquire food from gardens, usually intended for birds.

cached food resources, rather than just the squirrel that buried them. They locate them by smelling the ground in likely places, as opposed to using their memory, so all individuals will have a rough idea of where to begin looking.

Hazel dormice stash food away too. In the wild, they amass hazel nuts in dry and sheltered places, such as the crevices between coppiced tree branches or in tree cavities. In gardens, they will often use spare nest boxes for this purpose, so it is a good idea to install a number of boxes in order to make the habitat as attractive as possible. With the right habitat, adequate accommodation and a local population, it is quite likely that hazel dormice will take up residence.

Both the hazel dormouse and the edible dormouse hibernate between October and April. The hazel dormouse, being smaller, is unable to accumulate sufficient fat for the duration, so it will occasionally feed from its larder. The edible dormouse puts on so much fat that it becomes quite rotund, which is why the ancient Romans regarded it a choice food. They kept the animals in earthenware jars with plenty of chestnuts and acorns to feed on, until they were ready for the table.

Neither of the squirrels hibernates. They inhabit nests, called dreys, built in the tree canopy, which they use for shelter. During particularly uncongenial weather they will remain inside for prolonged periods in winter, but they emerge to feed frequently during the day when conditions allow. This is when their buried caches of food are utilised. In the case of red squirrels, they can also feed from fir cones that remain on the tree, giving them a clear advantage over grey squirrels when there is snow on the ground.

▼ The scientific species name *vulgaris* means 'common' in Latin, indicating how widespread and familiar the red squirrel (*Sciurus vulgaris*) used to be. Although it has been displaced by the grey squirrel over much of Britain, the red squirrel still has healthy populations in areas where it is better suited to the habitat.

Flying mammals

Although bats are not pests, they are generally viewed unfavourably by the British public, because they resemble vermin and have secretive nocturnal habits. In fact, they are not related to rodents and they can do us a useful service by eating mosquitoes and midges.

All of the British bat species are insectivorous, which means that they eat insects and other invertebrates, such as spiders and harvestmen. Most of their prey is caught on the wing, so flying insects form the greater part of their diet. In addition to mosquitoes and midges, they consume crane flies, lacewings, moths and beetles.

Bats are unique among British mammals in their ability to fly. Even more remarkably, they are able to fly and hunt in complete darkness, without injuring themselves by colliding with obstacles. They do this by echolocation, which means that they use echoes to locate objects in their flight path. They emit series of high-pitched clicking sounds from their mouths, which bounce off surfaces and return to their ears. The tiny differences in the time it takes for the clicks to return enables bats to build audio images of their surroundings, in much the same way that our eyes enable us to build visual images by using reflected light. Some bats have elaborate ears and masks, which are designed to channel the sound waves more efficiently.

As bats need to roost in places safe from predators, they are unable to migrate for the winter when their insect food is unavailable, so they hibernate instead. Their metabolism slows down to save energy and they remain in a state of torpor until springtime. Their hibernation roosts are often in caves and mine shafts, where they are protected from the worst weather conditions. During the breeding season they need to be near to feeding grounds, so they use temporary roosts instead. The females tend to roost separately in nursery roosts in large trees or roof apexes, where they give birth and nurture their young. The males need less room, so they are able to roost in smaller cavities in trees, behind bark, between wall stones and so on.

Female bats need to fly while they are pregnant, so they produce just one offspring per year, which is a very low rate of reproduction for small mammals. As a result, bats live for an extraordinarily long time for their size so that they are able to maintain their populations: 20–30 years. Nevertheless, they have been significantly reduced in numbers due to loss of feeding habitat and roosting sites. As a result, all bats are now protected by law, whether common or rare, because they often roost side by side.

This creates a curious paradox for those thinking of installing bat roosts in their gardens, as only bat-licensed ecologists are able to inspect the roosts when bats have taken up residence. That shouldn't deter people from doing so, however, as bats can still be enjoyed by watching them leave and return to their roosts, and watching them flitting about in the night sky. In addition, an electronic bat detector

▲ The most common and widespread of the British species, the common pipistrelle bat (*Pipistrellus pipistrellus*) is one of the vesper or evening bats, often seen hunting silhouetted against the sky at dusk.

can be used to listen to their echolocation calls, which are otherwise inaudible to most human ears due to their high frequency.

There are 17 bat species known to live in Britain. Some are rare and localised, while others are common and ubiquitous, with the rest somewhere in between. There is always the potential for bats to frequent our gardens, if we make the effort to provide better habitat for hunting insects and better facilities for roosting, both for breeding females and for itinerant males.

▼ Seen here roosting behind a window shutter, the male lesser noctule bat (*Nyctalus leisleri*) uses temporary roosts during the summer months, but in winter hibernates in places where it is better protected from the weather.

▲ The lesser horseshoe bat (*Rhinolophus hipposideros*) has an elaborate nose-leaf to aid in echolocation. It hunts for prey on the foliage and bark of trees as well as pursuing airborne insects.

◤ Bats vary greatly in facial form because they are adapted to fill subtly different econiches. The long-eared bat (*Plecotus auritus*) uses its enormous ears to detect small flying insects in which other bats are not interested.

▶ The common noctule bat (*Nyctalus noctula*) is among the largest of Britain's bat species. It often hunts for prey among swifts and swallows in the early evening, which may afford it some protection from falcons.

▼ Many bats roost by squeezing themselves into small spaces, but the greater horseshoe bat (*Rhinolophus ferrumequinum*) hangs in open spaces, shrouded by its wings and looking much like the popular image of a typical bat.

▼ Seen here roosting behind a shutter, Brandt's bat (*Myotis brandti*) has a thick pelt so that it can cope with the chilly nights that often come with sunny weather.

◀ The common shrew (*Sorex araneus*) is widespread in Britain, although absent from Ireland. It uses its long snout in a similar manner to a pig, by nosing through humus in search of prey, which it identifies by smell. The lifespan of the common shrew is roughly 15 months, so the population is entirely replaced by a new generation each year.

Insectivorous mammals

Although the term 'insectivore' implies an exclusive diet of insects, the mammals described in this way actually eat a wide variety of other invertebrates too, including worms, molluscs, spiders, millipedes, centipedes and crustaceans. They will also eat other small vertebrates and the carrion of larger vertebrates on occasion. The term is no longer used to group these species scientifically, but it is still a convenient way to group them in popular books, because they share common characteristics as small terrestrial predatory mammals, even though they are more distantly related than once thought. Although bats are also insectivorous in diet, they have evolved from a quite different line to that of shrews, moles and hedgehogs.

There are two species of shrew commonly found in British gardens – the common shrew and the pygmy shrew. They are much alike in appearance, apart from the difference in size, which enables them to occupy slightly different econiches within the same habitat.

Shrews do not hibernate, as they are able to feed on a variety of ground-living invertebrates throughout the year. However, they will enter a state of torpor when conditions

▼ Unlike the common shrew, the pygmy shrew (*Sorex minutus*) is also found in Ireland. It is about two-thirds the size of the common shrew and one-third the weight. The pygmy shrew has the distinction of being Britain's smallest mammal.

▼ Although far less numerous than the common and pygmy shrews, the water shrew (*Neomys fodiens*) does occur in some gardens with large ponds or streams within or nearby. The water shrew is Britain's largest shrew species and has a distinctive pale underside. It has mildly toxic saliva to assist in killing aquatic prey more rapidly, before it has a chance to escape.

become particularly cold or wet in winter, to avoid the risk of dying from energy loss. Shrews have very high metabolism, which means that they expend a lot of energy for their size during normal activity. In turn, this means that they need to eat voraciously and frequently to stay alive. This equates to something like 80–90% of their bodyweight in food each day, depending on the prey they find and other factors, such as temperature and whether they are rearing young.

The mole feeds almost exclusively on earthworms, although it will also eat the subterranean larvae of beetles, moths and flies, as well as other invertebrates and small vertebrates which it encounters as it digs past the roots of plants. As earthworms can escape quite rapidly, moles have toxic saliva to paralyse them. Most of their tunnels act as galleries in which earthworms expose themselves. In order to find enough food, moles require extensive networks of these galleries, which is why they can leave so many piles of excavated earth above ground, which we call molehills. Like shrews, moles do not hibernate, as their food is generally available all year round.

The hedgehog has a more catholic diet than shrews and moles. As well as invertebrates, hedgehogs will consume carrion, birds' eggs, berries, fruits and so on. As a result, they can be tempted into the open in gardens by offerings of food. There is a curious tradition of offering bread and milk to hedgehogs, which they will happily take, but they are better off with scraps of meat, hens' eggs or pet food. As hedgehogs are larger than shrews and moles, and they are able to eat foods containing higher levels of lipids and carbohydrates, this means they are able to put on fat reserves in the autumn months and then hibernate over winter. By doing so, it enables them to avoid uncongenial

▲ Although the mole (*Talpa europaea*) spends most of its life below ground, it will occasionally come to the surface if it needs to travel to new ground. This may be to find a mate, to claim new territory, to find food or to evacuate its domain due to the ground flooding, freezing or drying out.

weather conditions and to avoid predation from hungry badgers, thereby improving their overall chances of survival. In the wild, hedgehogs hibernate in nests made in old animal burrows or beneath fallen logs and so on. Hibernation boxes are certainly worth installing in gardens, and may prevent hedgehogs from nesting beneath bonfires and compost heaps, where they might come to an unfortunate end in the springtime, by fire or fork.

▼ The hedgehog (*Erinaceous europaeus*) uses its spines as an effective defence against most predators, but the badger is able to use its long front claws to unroll the hedgehog and bite into its unprotected belly.

The common rabbit (*Oryctolagus cuniculus*) is often regarded as a pest by gardeners, especially those who have vegetable patches, as these offer the animals a veritable banquet of foods that draw them like a magnet.

Meadow mammals

For those fortunate enough to have gardens visited – or even inhabited – by wild grazing mammals, it is fair to say that such animals are a mixed blessing. While they are pleasant to see on our lawns, they can certainly do a good deal of damage by foraging flowers and shrubs. This doesn't just apply to cultivated species and vegetables, but also to those planted with the intention of attracting wildlife. So it isn't necessarily a good thing to have rabbits and deer, unless there is sufficient area for their grazing and foraging to make little difference. On the positive side, their droppings add to the fertility and fecundity of wilderness patches, and the burrows of rabbits can be used by other small mammals, as well as social insects such as bumblebees and wasps.

As regards rabbits, in the context of a garden it is largely a matter of numbers. A few rabbits may be manageable, but too many can upset the ecological balance by denuding the habitat of greenery and its invertebrate community. It therefore falls to the individual to make a judgement about how to manage their rabbit population, especially as they famously have a habit of multiplying rather rapidly.

Although similar in appearance to rodents, the common rabbit belongs to a separate family named lagomorphs, along with the brown hare, which is an animal of open fields. The rabbit is known to have evolved in the western Mediterranean region and been introduced to Britain by the invading Romans in the first century AD. It was a valued source of food, because it was easily reared in captivity and would readily convert indigestible plant matter into meat. Its ability to proliferate also made it highly adaptable by offering many genetic variations for natural selection to work with. As a result, it quickly adapted to the British climate once it had escaped into the wild. Two thousand years on and it has become a quintessential part of the British landscape.

In order to acquire sufficient nutrition, deer eat a wide variety of plants, including grasses, herbs, flowers, shrubs and trees, as well as their seeds, fruits and berries. In fact, there are relatively few plants that deer avoid, which means

that they can leave a garden depleted of its flora if allowed to browse at will.

The roe deer is the most common of our native deer species and the most likely to be found in British gardens. It is a medium-sized deer with relatively small antlers and no tail, which are adaptations for escaping predators – long since extinct – through thicket and forest. In the summer it has a chestnut brown pelt, which turns greyish in the winter. The roe deer is known for its athletic ability at leaping very high obstacles, which means that it sometimes enters and exits gardens over surprisingly tall fences and hedges. It is a graceful and elegant creature, perfectly evolved for life in forest and clearing.

The fallow deer is rather less beautifully proportioned than the roe deer, and rather less flowing in its movements. Like the rabbit, the fallow deer was introduced to Britain by the Romans in the first century AD as livestock. It has far larger antlers than the roe deer, with a larger head to take the additional stresses and strains. It also has shorter legs and a generally more robust frame. It consequently carries more meat than the roe deer, which is why the Romans favoured it as a food animal. Its pelage is pale below and brown above, with a spangled pattern that provides cryptic camouflage by mimicking dappled sunlight penetrating the forest canopy. Fallow deer are more often found in herds than roe deer, which tend to be seen alone, or in pairs or small groups. As they are less streamlined and athletic, fallow deer are less likely to enter gardens, unless they have clear points of access and egress.

There are other introduced deer species in Britain. The most widespread and likely to be seen in gardens is the muntjac, a primitive deer originating from Asia which escaped from zoological collections in the UK and has now established a healthy population. It is a small, stocky, almost boar-like deer, well designed for skulking in thick undergrowth. It is essentially nocturnal, although it can sometimes be seen in the daytime. Males have small horn-like antlers, fang-like incisor teeth and striped heads.

▲ Although related to the common rabbit, the brown hare (*Lepus europaeus*) is a very different animal. It is adapted for fast running, as it does not dig burrows to escape from predators. It prefers open country so that it can see danger approaching.

▲ Deer fawns, including those of the fallow deer (*Dama dama*), are born precocial, which means that they are ready to walk and follow their parents. Many other mammals have altricial young, meaning they are born naked and blind and require nurturing in a nest or den.

▶ The rump of the roe deer (*Capreolus capreolus*) has a conspicuous white patch, called a flash. The purpose of the flash is to enable the deer to remain in visual contact with one another when they are roaming in shadowy forest or fleeing from predators.

▼ The name 'muntjac' is derived from the Indonesian, meaning 'small deer', as the muntjac (*Muntiacus reevesi*) is indeed very small in relation to other deer. It is perfectly suited to a secretive life among the bushes.

◢ The scientific name for the red deer (*Cervus elaphus*) is both Latin and Greek. *Cervus* is Latin for deer, and *elaphus* is Greek for deer, making it the quintessential deer, with its large size and impressive antlers.

▲ The sika deer (*Cervus nippon*) is a smaller relative of the red deer, originally from southern Asia, including Japan – hence its species name *nippon*. Like other non-native deer species, it has escaped from zoological collections.

▲ Another escapee, the water deer (*Hydropotes inermis*) has become common in some areas of Britain, especially in marshy habitats, to which it is adapted. It has no antlers but large canine teeth, which are especially pronounced in the male.

Opportunist mammals

As a measure of their adaptability, both the fox and the badger have been labelled with the prefixes 'urban' and 'rural' in recognition of the fact that they now have populations in our towns and cities as well as in the countryside. This is because both species are opportunist feeders with omnivorous diets. In their natural habitat they exploit all kinds of animal and plant foods, but in a man-made habitat they exploit the wide variety of scraps that people leave in their bins, drop on the street or leave out for the birds. Of course, some people intentionally feed urban foxes and badgers too, while the animals will also take advantage of the bounty to be found at waste depots and landfill sites.

Despite their similarity in lifestyle, the two species are not closely related, as the fox belongs to the canid family, along with dogs and wolves, while the badger belongs to the mustelid family, along with weasels, martens and otters. Both are largely nocturnal and live below ground – the fox in a lair and the badger in a sett. In fact, foxes will often use abandoned badger setts or evict their tenants, as they are not so well equipped for digging. Where no badger setts are available, they may dig beneath large trees or utilise the voids underneath garden sheds and so on.

Inevitably, people have mixed feelings about foxes and badgers living in, or passing through, their gardens. Foxes are famous for their bloodlust and will readily kill domestic animals, such as chickens, ducks, rabbits and guinea pigs. Badgers are less likely to kill livestock, but they will eat hedgehogs and excavate a lawn in search of worms and other invertebrates. Both will also steal food put out for

▼ The killer instinct in the fox (*Vulpes vulpes*) is so strong that it will readily attack domestic fowl and small livestock. If it gets the chance to catch more than one prey animal in the wild, it will do so and stash the surplus away, which is why it doesn't know when to stop killing in a chicken coop.

other animals and raid bird nests for their eggs and chicks. In many cases it is a matter of learning to tolerate their presence and physically deterring them from entering places where they are not welcome.

This might be thought of as wildlife management, so that we only have ourselves to blame if they are allowed to cause damage and destruction, because they cannot help their innate behaviour. There is always a danger of *anthropomorphising* animals, which means judging their behaviour by human standards, as if they have the ability to make choices based on our sense of right and wrong or good and bad. Unfortunately, nature doesn't work that way, so it falls to us to understand that foxes and badgers are ruled by instincts, and to adapt our own behaviour accordingly to prevent them from reacting to those instincts, if that is what we desire.

It is also worth mentioning the domestic cat here. There are two schools of thought on this matter. Whilst it is indubitably true that cats kill many small garden mammals and birds, it is also true that those mammals and birds have relatively few natural predators, due to the human impact on the landscape, especially in urban areas. As a consequence the domestic cat can be viewed as a necessary ecological stand-in, so that natural selection can rid resident urban populations of individuals that are physically or behaviourally aberrant, and therefore keep species genetically honed for survival, as would happen in the wild.

It is worth remembering that the cat was originally domesticated precisely because it was an efficient predator of vermin, so the same characteristic is still proving useful even though we may not be aware of it in the context of the bigger picture, because we tend to focus on the smaller picture. Nature is all about the fine balance between life and death, because that is what drives and steers the unsentimental process of natural selection. What is anthropomorphically perceived as cruelty in the cat's instincts, when it catches and mortally toys with a small animal, is actually a contribution to the continued survival of that animal's species as a whole. Foxes and badgers can be regarded in the same light, as they too will readily take wild animals that do not, or cannot, evade their attentions. They will also, like the cat, instinctively kill without eating their prey if their appetite is already sated, though this is less likely to happen.

With a little patience it is possible to coax foxes and badgers into the open in gardens, where we can enjoy watching them feed, play and squabble. The trick to this is to frequently and regularly offer food in the same place after dark, and to make the creatures feel relaxed by avoiding any sudden movements, abrupt noises or bright lights. Wild animals will only eat and drink when entirely calm, because they need to compromise their senses when they feed. This can be particularly rewarding when adults are accompanied by cubs, as they are always more appealing, both in appearance and behaviour.

▲ The badger (*Meles meles*) has poor eyesight because of its subterranean lifestyle, where smell and hearing are more useful. The conspicuous white stripes make the badgers highly visible to one another in the darkness, both inside and outside of the sett, which helps them communicate.

▼ The domestic cat is descended from the wildcat (*Felis sylvestris*), which still exists in some remote European locations, including parts of Scotland. The domestic cat exhibits a phenomenon known as behavioural neoteny, which means that it retains infantile behaviour in the adult. This is why it will play with its prey like a kitten and begin to knead and purr when it is being stroked. Humans have artificially selected neoteny in both cats and dogs, because the trait makes them more affectionate and dependent as pets.

▲ The stoat (*Mustela erminea*) has relatively poor eyesight, because it is adapted to hunting by using its senses of smell and hearing, along burrows and through thick undergrowth, where its eyes are kept closed to protect them.

▼ The most noticeable thing about the weasel (*Mustela nivalis*) is how small it is. As it is adapted to hunting small rodents it has similar dimensions, except that its body and neck have become elongated.

Small hunters

Stoats and weasels are members of the Mustelid family, along with badgers, martens, otters and polecats. They are essentially different-sized versions of the same animal, so they fill slightly different econiches within the same environment by preying on different animals. Both species have an elongated body design, which enables them to chase prey down burrows. If the head will enter a burrow then the body can follow, so they will chase their quarry down surprisingly tight tunnels.

For their size they are quite vicious, and will think nothing of dispatching animals considerably larger than themselves. Weasels will tackle small mammals ranging from voles to rats, while stoats will go for prey as large as squirrels and rabbits. They will similarly prey on birds appropriate to their size, especially ground-nesting species. In order to deal with their victims with minimal risk of injury and loss of energy, they seize the neck with a vice-like bite and hold on until the death throes cease.

Stoats and weasels inhabit dens, which are usually situated in banks, beneath tree roots or within decaying tree stumps and fallen trunks. Females require appropriately sized cavities for nesting, but both sexes use a number of dens in rotation throughout a territory, so that sufficient numbers of prey can be caught. When the kittens begin to venture out of the nesting den and explore their surroundings they do so in sibling gangs and are sometimes seen horse-playing together with their mothers. This play behaviour enables young stoats and weasels to develop and refine their coordination and hunting skills, ultimately enabling them to fend for themselves.

Apart from the size difference, which isn't always evident in the field, the best way to distinguish between the stoat and the weasel is to look at the tail. The stoat has a proportionately longer tail with a black tip, while the weasel's is uniform fulvous-brown. Size can also be confusing, because males are larger than females, so that a male weasel can be almost the same size as a female stoat. Unlike the weasel, the stoat will sometimes turn white in winter, but only in the northern reaches of its range, where it serves as camouflage in snow. There are intermediate forms too, but its southern form remains brown above. Those of the white form are known as ermine and the fur was once used to adorn the cloaks and hats of royalty.

Stoats and weasels are found in both urban and rural gardens, because their prey is found there too. They will also respond to being fed by humans with scraps of meat. As they are both rather diminutive in size, compared with badgers and foxes, it is more convenient to install den boxes for them if desired. They may use these as temporary accommodation, during their hunting rounds, or for nesting. It goes without saying that resident stoats or weasels may have a detrimental effect on other garden wildlife, either by eating it scaring it away, so they probably suit a large garden best.

▲ So called because it looks rather like a cat stretched into a pole-shape, the polecat (*Mustela putorius*) is the species from which domesticated ferrets are descended. It occasionally visits gardens to scavenge food but is very secretive.

◄ The pine marten (*Martes martes*) is an arboreal member of the weasel family. It is a scarce and shy creature, but it does visit gardens to take food in places where populations remain in areas of ancient woodland.

◄ An escapee from fur farms, the American mink (*Neovison vison*) is an invasive species in Britain and has caused problems by preying on water voles and ground-nesting water birds, such as the water rail. It will sometimes make passing visits through large gardens with ponds or streams.

▼ In recent years the otter (*Lutra lutra*) has made a significant comeback in numbers, because it is no longer persecuted by river wardens. It is therefore far more likely to be seen visiting large garden ponds, where the captive fish make an easy meal.

Terrestrial rodents

Voles are similar to mice in many respects, but they are adapted for a life spent in tunnels below sward, undergrowth and leaf-litter. Their blunt noses enable voles to push their way through the plant debris and detritus, leaving tunnels as they go, which they will often line with moss. They use their tunnels as thoroughfares to link their nests with places to feed, latrines and so on, whilst remaining hidden from predators, such as weasels and owls. As they seldom climb, voles have no requirement for a long tail as a counterbalance, so it has become a stub to prevent predators from grabbing it. They also have small ears, to prevent them from being damaged as they run through their tunnels. As a consequence voles have a rather squat and rounded appearance.

There are three species that might be encountered in British gardens – the common vole, the field vole and the bank vole. They are much alike in appearance and habits. They are all essentially vegetarian, eating roots, shoots, seeds, berries etc, but they will also eat insects and other invertebrates to supplement their diets. Predation and harsh winters can reduce vole numbers considerably, but they are able to produce large litters in several seasonal broods, enabling their populations to recover very quickly. Ground-level nest boxes can be used to attract voles into gardens. They will also nest underneath old sheets of corrugated iron or other warm and dry places that they can enter and exit via their safety tunnels.

Although mice and rats are fundamentally terrestrial or ground-living in design, they are also fairly good at climbing. They have longer limbs and tails than voles, to enable them to scale obstacles and to balance as they reach from one foothold to another. This means that they are able to exploit a different econiche from voles. In addition, mice and rats come in a range of sizes, so that they are each adapted to exploit slightly different aspects of that econiche. Mice and rats are more omnivorous in their diets than voles and they are also more opportunistic, making them well suited to urban environments where survival is often a matter of making the most of what's on offer. This includes morsels of food left in bins, on the street, beneath bird tables and so on.

There are three species of mouse likely to be found in British gardens – the wood mouse, the yellow-necked mouse and the house mouse – and two species of rat – the black rat and the brown rat. The wood mouse and yellow-necked mouse are indigenous to the British Isles, while the other three are invasive species: the house mouse came across the English Channel with Neolithic people in prehistoric times, while the black rat arrived with the Romans and the brown rat arrived at the turn of the 18th century. Effectively, these three species introduced themselves to Britain by stowing away on boats along with cargoes. Due to this close association with humans it follows that they are the most frequently encountered in urban gardens.

The wood mouse and yellow-necked mouse are more often found in rural gardens, as they are adapted to the natural woodland and hedgerow habitats of Britain. There are urban populations, though, as they do well in parks and other areas of 'urban wilderness' such as river and canal banks. Any urban gardens adjacent to these may well harbour wood mice and yellow-necked mice.

Of course, the house mouse, black rat and brown rat are generally considered to be vermin, as they are known to spread germs and disease, but the wood mouse and yellow-necked mouse do not pose the same problem. So it is certainly worth considering the installation of nest boxes. If they are some distance away from the house and other artificial sources of food, such as rubbish and compost bins, then they shouldn't attract the unwelcome species.

▶ The common vole (*Microtus arvalis*) can indeed be very common. As its reproductive cycle is short it can fit several broods into a season, so that its population can swell to plague proportions in favourable years. The fluctuations in vole numbers has a knock-on effect with regard to the success of predatory birds, mammals and reptiles.

▲ The field vole (*Microtus agrestis*) is smaller than the common vole and has a relatively short tail. As its name suggests, the field vole is more likely to be found in open meadow, although it needs plenty of close ground cover to avoid predation.

▶ The bank vole (*Myodes glareolus*) is a similar size to the field vole, but it has a longer tail and noticeably more prominent ears, much like a mouse. While the other voles are greyish-brown in colour, the bank vole has a chestnut brown back.

▼ As its long tail indicates, the wood mouse (*Apodemus sylvaticus*) is particularly good at climbing and jumping. The tail is used as a counterbalance to stabilise the mouse as it reaches or leaps between gaps.

◣ With longer limbs and longer tail, the yellow-necked mouse (*Apodemus flavicollis*) is even better adapted to a semi-arboreal lifestyle than the wood mouse. It can therefore fill a slightly different econiche.

▲ Although more likely to be seen inside buildings than outside, the house mouse (*Mus musculus*) will go al fresco in summer months to exploit available garden resources, such as invertebrates, seeds, fruits and so on.

▲ In terms of size, the black rat (*Rattus rattus*) falls between the brown rat and mice. It is less well suited to cold climates than the brown rat, and is very scarce in Britain.

◄ As its scientific name alludes, the brown rat (*Rattus norvegicus*) was erroneously thought to have arrived in Britain via Norway, on trading ships. In fact the species did not arrive in Norway until many years later.

◣ In larger gardens with ponds or streams within or nearby, it is possible that the water vole (*Arvicola amphibious*) may be seen, although it has become rather rare due to predation by American mink. Being a large vole, it is sometimes incorrectly described as the water rat.

▼ The harvest mouse (*Micromys minutus*) is sometimes found in rural gardens following harvests, when it finds itself homeless and in search of suitable habitat. The species is a victim of modern farming methods, as mechanisation destroys the animals before they have a chance to escape to the hedgerows.

Although squirrels are tree-dwelling rodents, they also spend a good deal of time on the ground, where they find much of their food.

BAT ROOST BOX

Kit

For this project you will need a general toolkit, as suggested on page 14. The project is designed to make it easy for you to measure and cut the components, and to assemble the pieces. The project uses 12mm plywood and standard roofing batten, but you can improvise with similar materials.

Instructions:

1 Screw or nail the four longer lengths of batten to the back plate to make a frame.

2 Secure the shorter lengths of batten to the back plate to create a crawl space when the front plate is placed on top. Leave an even gap around the front plate for the bats to enter and exit.

3 Fix some thick plastic sheet (polythene or damp proof course) with clout nails to provide protection from the rain.

4 Now drill holes in the top and bottom sections of the back plate and fix your bat roost box to a tree or wall in a shady and quiet spot.

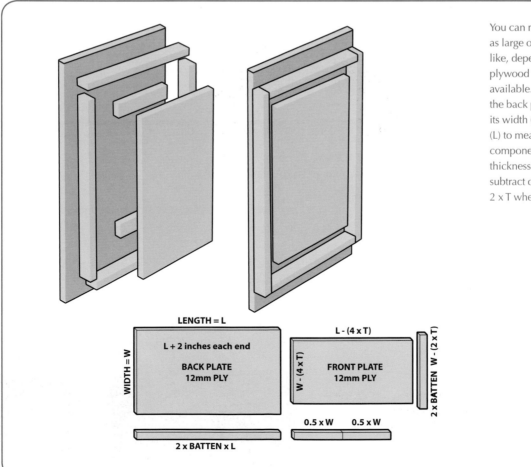

You can make this project as large or small as you like, depending on the plywood you have available. Once you have the back plate cut, then use its width (W) and its length (L) to measure the other components. T = the thickness of the batten, so subtract or minus (-) 4, 3 or 2 x T where it says.

LENGTH = L

WIDTH = W

L + 2 inches each end

BACK PLATE
12mm PLY

2 x BATTEN x L

L - (4 x T)

W - (4 x T)

FRONT PLATE
12mm PLY

2 x BATTEN W - (2 x T)

0.5 x W   0.5 x W

NOT TO SCALE

BAT NURSERY BOX

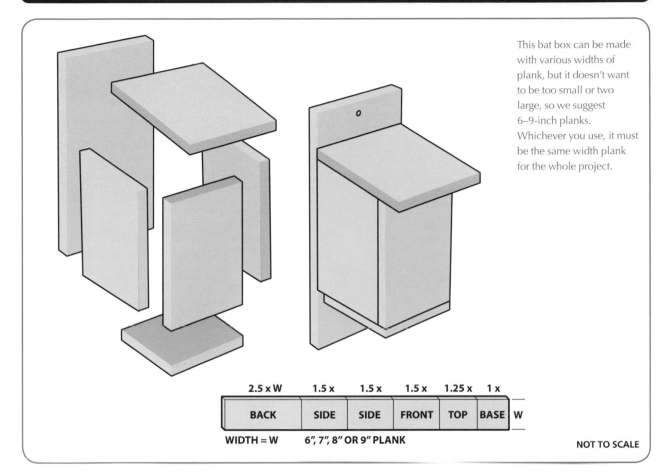

This bat box can be made with various widths of plank, but it doesn't want to be too small or two large, so we suggest 6–9-inch planks. Whichever you use, it must be the same width plank for the whole project.

2.5 x W	1.5 x	1.5 x	1.5 x	1.25 x	1 x
BACK	SIDE	SIDE	FRONT	TOP	BASE

W

WIDTH = W   **6", 7", 8" OR 9" PLANK**

NOT TO SCALE

Kit

For this project you will need a standard toolkit, as listed on page 14. In addition to your chosen plank size, you will also need some polythene or damp proof course (dpc) as a rain covering. The project is designed to make it easy for you to measure and cut the components, and to assemble the pieces. Always be careful with sharp tools.

Instructions:

1 Using screws or nails, attach the side panels to the back plate, making sure they are exactly the same height, by using a set-square.
2 Fix the front panel to the side panels.
3 Secure the top panel in place.
4 Rough-up the inside surfaces of the box with a chisel, or glue some tree bark or twigs inside, to give the bats a better grip.
5 Fit the base panel, leaving a gap to the rear, so that the bats can enter and exit the box from below.
6 Add some polythene or dpc with clout nails as a rain cover - as seen in the photo.
7 Drill holes in the back plate and mount your box in a sheltered spot, on a tree or a wall.

SMALL MAMMAL BOX – SUSPENDED

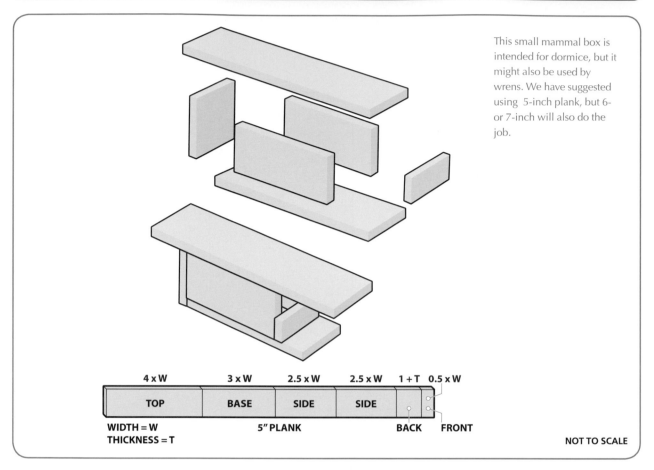

This small mammal box is intended for dormice, but it might also be used by wrens. We have suggested using 5-inch plank, but 6- or 7-inch will also do the job.

4 x W	3 x W	2.5 x W	2.5 x W	1 + T	0.5 x W
TOP	BASE	SIDE	SIDE		

WIDTH = W
THICKNESS = T
5" PLANK
BACK   FRONT

NOT TO SCALE

Kit:

Please refer to page 14 for the general tool kit you are likely to need for this project. The project is designed to make it easy for you to measure and cut the components, and to assemble the pieces. Always be careful with sharp tools. In addition to the plank of wood, you will also need something to protect the box from the weather, such as polythene, and some long cable ties for securing it beneath a suitable branch, as shown in the photo.

Instructions:

1 Screw or nail the side panels to the base, making sure they align with the back edge.
2 Secure the back panel, making sure the top edge is flush with the sides.
3 Fit the top panel to create a roof, making sure that it extends to the front and rear of the box.
4 Fix the front panel to reduce the size of the entrance.
5 Use clout nails to position some polythene or damp proof course as protection from rain.
6 Use long cable ties (or short ones linked together) to strap the box beneath a suitable branch, where cats and other predators cannot reach the entrance.

SMALL MAMMAL BOX – MOUNTED

Kit:

For most of the build, you will need a basic tool kit, as described on page 14. You will also need to use a hole-cutter, so be sure to do this safely, by clamping the panel properly and wearing safety goggles. The project is designed to make it easy for you to measure and cut the components, and to assemble the pieces. In addition to the plank of wood, you will also need some polythene as weather proofing.

Instructions:

1 Carefully measure and cut the entrance hole in the back panel before assembly.
2 Use screws or nails to fix the side panels to the back panel. Make sure they are level by using a set-square.
3 Fit the front panel and then the top and bottom panels.
4 Use polythene and clout nails to weatherproof the top of the box.
5 Drill fixing holes in the top and bottom of the back panel, making sure they are off-centre, so the entrance hole can be set to one side.
6 Mount the box to a suitable tree trunk , low to the ground or above a fork.

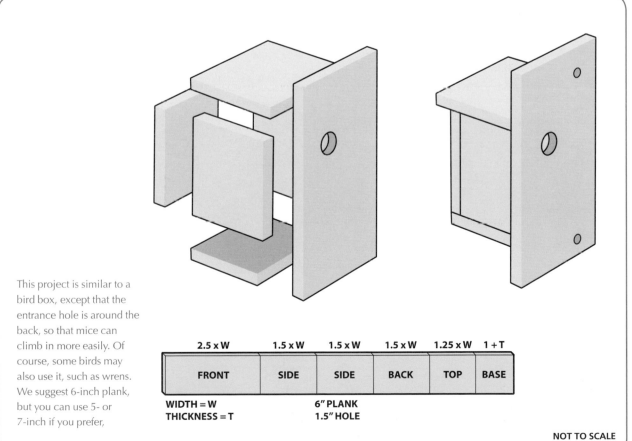

This project is similar to a bird box, except that the entrance hole is around the back, so that mice can climb in more easily. Of course, some birds may also use it, such as wrens. We suggest 6-inch plank, but you can use 5- or 7-inch if you prefer,

2.5 x W	1.5 x W	1.5 x W	1.5 x W	1.25 x W	1 + T
FRONT	SIDE	SIDE	BACK	TOP	BASE

WIDTH = W   6" PLANK
THICKNESS = T   1.5" HOLE

NOT TO SCALE

MEDIUM MAMMAL BOX – FRONT ENTRY

Kit:

In addition to the usual tool kit, as shown on page 14, it is necessary to use a large hole cutter for the entrance to the box. This should be done with the necessary safety precautions in mind. Due to the friction, the best approach is to cut the hole gradually, by moving the cutter up and down. This clears the blade to stop it from jamming or burning the wood. This job must be done by an adult, as it requires strength and control.

Instructions:

1 Screw or nail the side panels to the base panel, making sure the ends are flush.

2 Fix the back and front panels, making sure the top edges are flush – the entrance hole must be cut prior to fitting.

3 Fit the top panel, leaving a lip and the front to provide some shelter.

4 Use clout nails to secure a polythene or DPC roof covering.

5 Place the box in a suitable place, well hidden away.

This box is essentially for hedgehogs, although it is possible that stoats or weasels may use it too. It needs to be tucked away in the undergrowth, so that it simulates a cavity in the ground.

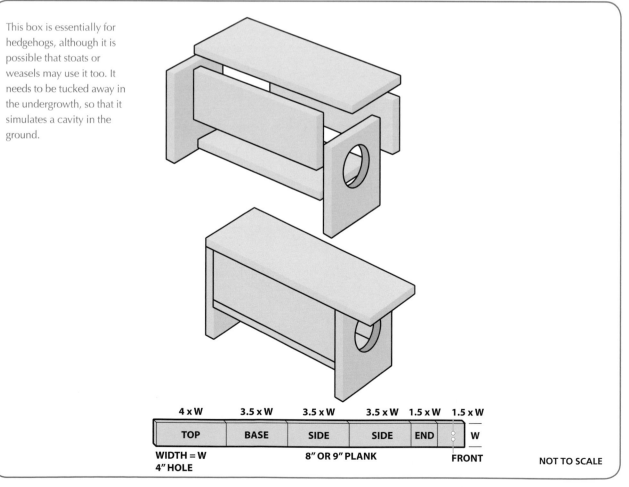

4 x W	3.5 x W	3.5 x W	3.5 x W	1.5 x W	1.5 x W
TOP	BASE	SIDE	SIDE	END	W

WIDTH = W   8" OR 9" PLANK   FRONT
4" HOLE

NOT TO SCALE

MEDIUM MAMMAL BOX – SIDE ENTRY

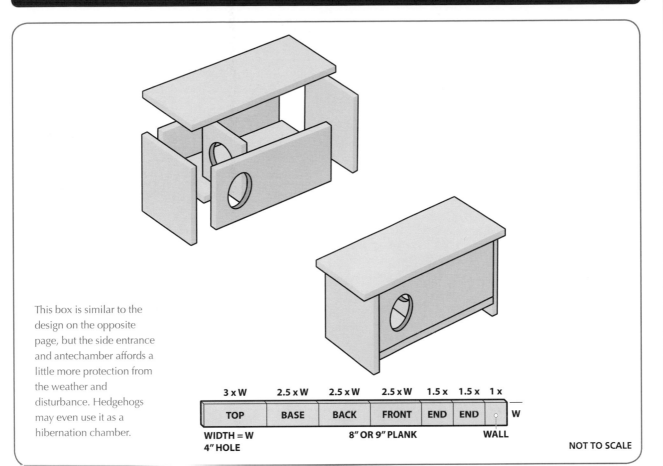

This box is similar to the design on the opposite page, but the side entrance and antechamber affords a little more protection from the weather and disturbance. Hedgehogs may even use it as a hibernation chamber.

3 x W	2.5 x W	2.5 x W	2.5 x W	1.5 x	1.5 x	1 x	
TOP	BASE	BACK	FRONT	END	END		W

WIDTH = W   8" OR 9" PLANK   WALL
4" HOLE

NOT TO SCALE

Kit:

As with the previous design, this project requires a hole cutter in addition to the usual selection of tools. This time, two holes are required. It is always best to cut holes in larger pieces of plank and then trim them to size, as it provides something substantial to clamp down during the cutting procedure. Follow the same advice on cutting technique and make sure an adult does the job.

Instructions:

1 Use screws or nails to fix the front and back panels to the base panel.
2 Slide the wall panel between the front and back panels and secure in the appropriate place to leave the entrance hole clear.
3 Now fit the end panels, making sure the top edges are flush.
4 Finally position the roof or top panel.
5 Use clout nails to furnish the roof with a protective layer of polythene or DPC.
6 Place the box in an appropriate place, well hidden away – both types of box can be buried in leaf-litter or compost to enhance their appeal to animals.

BIRDS

Like mammals, birds are warm-blooded, but they differ from mammals in various ways. Instead of fur, birds have feathers as their body insulation. Feathers are structurally more useful than hairs too, which is how birds have evolved their ability to fly.

Birds reproduce by laying eggs in nests, where they are incubated by the parents until they hatch. Some species have altricial chicks, which means they require protection and feeding until they are ready to leave the nest. Other species have precocial chicks, which means they are able to see, walk and leave the nest in search of shelter and food.

Birds have adapted to various different animal diets, which include mammals, other birds, reptiles, amphibians, insects and other invertebrates. They have also adapted to various plant diets, which include leaves, shoots, berries and other fruits, nuts and seeds. Some bird species are residents, which means they remain in Britain throughout the year, while many others are migrants, which means they travel to and from Britain at certain times of the year. Some visit Britain in the summer, while others arrive in the winter.

Thicket-nesting birds

A number of birds build their nests in thickets, shrubbery or undergrowth, where they are well hidden from predators and protected from attack should a predator discover them. They usually build away from the ground to avoid terrestrial predators, but low enough to ensure that the thicket is dense enough for arboreal and flying predators to have difficulty getting close. When they visit their nests they are careful to alight some distance away and then wend their way closer under cover, so that predators cannot easily locate the nest site simply by watching the movements of the adults. There is always a compromise, though, as the birds need to get on with the business of breeding when food is available to feed their chicks, so quite a few perish because nests are found and raided. For this reason many birds are multi-brooded – meaning they have several broods in a season – so that they stand a better chance of seeing some of their chicks fledge the nest. Even if they do, the odds are still stacked against them surviving long enough to breed the following year; such is the ongoing struggle for survival and reproduction in nature.

There are generally two types of thicket nest: the cup nest and the ball nest. As their names suggest, they are defined by their respective shapes. The main body of these nests is constructed from small twigs, grass stems and so on, which are woven together to form the shape and to attach the nest to surrounding undergrowth. Once the main body is completed, the next consideration is comfort and warmth for the eggs and nestlings, so the nest is then lined with suitable materials, which may include pieces of moss and lichen, feathers, fine grasses, strands of cobweb, plant fibres, strands of wool and animal hairs or fur. Man-made materials may also be used, such as fragments of paper and plastic bag. Ball nests include a dome above the cup, which affords better protection from the elements and from predators, both physically and visually by providing cryptic camouflage. As the female birds spend more time on the nest, they too tend to have predominantly cryptic colouring, so that predators are less likely to notice them sitting on eggs or chicks.

Ground-nesting birds

In places where there are few trees and shrubs, or where the perceived threat from predators is from above, there are passerine, or perching, birds that habitually nest on or near to the ground. Some do so in open country, within grassy knolls or under scrub, while others do so at the margins, where hedgerow meets meadow or at the edge of water. They tend to make similar nests to those that build higher from the ground, but they are often not faced with the same structural challenges because their nests are supported by a bed of vegetation. In essence they are cups tipped on their side to allow access and egress from a particular vantage.

Ground-nesting, non-passerine birds usually build little more than a lined depression in the ground layer, whether it happens to be leaf litter, sandy soil, dry grass and so on. This is because they typically have *precocial* chicks, which means that

◀ Longtail tit nest.

▶ Pheasant nest.

▼ Song thrush nest.

they hatch ready to leave the nest, so that the nest doesn't need to function as a nursery. Passerine birds have *altricial* chicks, which means that they hatch less well developed and more dependent on their parents for warmth and food, so nests need to be better constructed and last longer.

Ledge-, recess- and cavity-nesting birds

The majority of garden birds instinctively choose to build their nests in cavities and recesses or on ledges. These occur naturally in trees, banks and precipices, but walls and buildings can also offer many suitable nesting opportunities, so that some species are associated with human habitations. Some birds also excavate their own nest holes from suitable surfaces, such as rotten tree stumps and earthen cliffs.

Demand may exceed availability of suitable nesting locations, and many birds will not breed if they cannot find places that satisfy their instincts. This is because compromising on nest sites is not worth the risk, as the chances are that their efforts at reproduction will end in failure and even in their own predation. The argument for providing a variety of nest boxes for all of these species is therefore a valid and strong one. As our walls, buildings and gardens tend to be too well kept and maintained to provide incidental nesting sites, it is necessary to intentionally cater for the needs of these birds if we expect to improve the ecological health of our garden habitats.

By and large, hole- and crevice-nesting birds have no need to put much effort into building their nests, because there is no requirement for structural support. They therefore tend to simply insert a lining made from warm and soft materials to cushion their eggs and provide comfort for their offspring. However, those birds that nest on and under ledges or eaves do, of course, require structure. As they are unable to attach their nests by weaving and tying them to surrounding objects, the solution is to use mud, reinforced with strands of plant and animal fibre. This natural 'wattle and daub' serves to provide shape and form to the nest, and to cement the nest in position. As long as the mud remains dry, then the nest will remain intact.

Bird families

Most garden birds are passerines, or perching birds. They share a mechanism in their legs, which causes them to close their toes together when their legs are pushed upwards as they alight on branches. This means that their own body weight ensures a tight grip when they perch, which is especially important when the birds are roosting at night. Their feet naturally let go of the perch when they jump and take to the air. The passerines range in size from the raven to the gold crest, but they tend to have a similar body form and arboreo-terrestrial lifestyle, which means that they divide their time between the trees and the ground. This is why so many passerine species are found in gardens, as most gardens are areas of open lawn surrounded by herbage, shrubbery and forest. In effect, this mimics the natural habitat of inland Britain in general, which is largely deciduous woodland interspersed with clearings and meadows.

Passerines: Tits

Easily the most familiar and quintessential garden birds are the tits. The great tit, blue tit and coal tit are widespread and common species in both rural and urban gardens, where they readily come to bird feeders and make use of nest boxes. They often forage among trees in mixed flocks, as this behaviour makes it more difficult for sparrowhawks to hunt them. It works as a survival strategy because there are more eyes on the lookout for danger, and movement en masse serves to confuse the predator, making it less able to single-out an individual and make a kill.

The long-tailed tit is also commonly seen in gardens but is less likely to breed there because it is not a cavity brooder, so doesn't use nest boxes. Instead it builds an ovoid nest in dense thicket, made from an elastic mixture of moss, lichen and spider webs. Two very similar species – the willow tit and the marsh tit – are also fairly widespread, but are often overlooked, because they are dowdy in colour and prefer more rural habitats, where they are more likely to nest in natural cavities.

Tits feed mainly on soft seeds, fruit and invertebrates, as is evident from their beaks, which are far more delicate than those of finches and buntings. They take full advantage of the summer glut of insects, larvae and spiders to produce multiple broods in order to bolster their numbers. This is important for survival, as harsh winters can deplete their populations considerably due to scarcity of food, cold temperatures and predation. There is a delicate balance involved, because fewer individuals might actually be more likely to survive because they will get more food between them, but they are more likely to fall prey before the next breeding season arrives.

Winter food consists mainly of very small hibernating invertebrates hiding on the trunks, branches and twigs of trees. This is why bird tables and feeders are so attractive to tits, as a couple of visits might easily provide a better meal than a bird can find naturally over a whole day. Foods such as peanuts and suet offer high carbohydrate morsels, which are exactly what a bird needs to generate sufficient warmth to avoid hypothermia and energy to evade the attentions of predators.

▼ The blue tit (*Parus caeruleus*) has been known to nest inside patio heaters, post boxes, litter bins and so on. This nesting adaptability has made the blue tit one of the most iconic of British garden birds.

▼ When the great tit (*Parus major*) appears at a bird table or feeder, the other species of tit instinctively make way. If they didn't then the great tit would make it quite clear they needed to wait their turn.

▲ As it looks rather like a smaller and drabber version of the great tit, the coal tit (*Parus ater*) is often overlooked in our gardens. It is identified easily by a small patch of white on the nape of the neck.

◣ The long-tailed tit (*Aegithalos caudatus*) belongs to a different genus from the other tit species. It lacks the dark cap on top of its head and it has a proportionately long tail as a balance to enable it to lean forwards on twigs in search of food.

▶ Together with the willow tit, the marsh tit (*Parus palustris*) is a tidy but rather nondescript-looking bird. In the field the two species are rather difficult to separate visually, but they have different calls.

▼ The willow tit (*Parus montanus*) has a proportionately larger head than the marsh tit, extending further down the back. The black cap also meets the brown of the back squarely, while that of the marsh tit tapers to a point.

▼ Where the crested tit (*Parus cristatus*) occurs, in Scotland, it can be a common sight in gardens. The other tits can raise and flatten their caps to express emotions, but this tit has evolved a conspicuous crest because it lives in dark conifer forests.

▲ The nuthatch (*Sitta europaea*) is a handsome-looking bird, with its streamlined shape and the contrast between its glaucous and peach colouring, above and below. It can sometime be heard hammering to get at wood-boring insect larvae.

▼ In marked contrast to the nuthatch, the treecreeper (*Certhia familiaris*) is cryptically camouflaged. This is because the bird roosts by wedging itself in crevices between tree bark, so the camouflage keeps it hidden from predators.

Passerines: Nuthatch and treecreeper

These two species are not closely related, but they live alongside one another because their habits have filled slightly different econiches within the same habitat, so they avoid direct competition with one another. Both hunt primarily for invertebrates on or under the bark of large trees, but they do so in quite different ways. For one thing, the nuthatch tends to start at the top of a tree trunk and work its way downwards, while the treecreeper starts at the bottom and works its way upwards. As a result, they each spot items of food that the other does not, entirely due to the angle of inspection.

They also have different beaks. The nuthatch has a straight and chisel-like beak, very much like that of a woodpecker, which it can use to poke around beneath pieces of loose bark and rotten wood to access invertebrates otherwise hidden from view. The treecreeper has a slender and decurved beak, which it can use to hook out invertebrates secreted in deep and narrow crevices and cracks. So both species can reach invertebrates that the other cannot. The nuthatch, as its name suggests, will also use its bill to eat nuts and seeds, and will often come to bird feeders.

As both the nuthatch and treecreeper naturally nest in cavities, they will also use nest boxes. Nuthatches have the unusual habit of adjusting the size of the entrance with mud until they achieve a snug fit. This seems to help in deterring would-be predators and other birds that may be interested in commandeering the nest site for their own use. Treecreepers prefer a nest box with a tapered cavity and side entrance, so that it mimics the natural cleavages they would ordinarily use in the wild.

Passerines: Wren and goldcrest

The jury is still out as to which of these birds is the smallest British species, both in terms of weight and length. The truth, of course, is that specimens vary in size, so that one would need to measure many individuals to find a mean average for each species and make a comparison. Both species are such a diminutive size because they specialise in hunting for invertebrates in dense thicket and canopy, where other birds are too big to fit through the gaps. As well as providing an econiche, this also affords protection from sparrowhawks, as they cannot penetrate the thickest tangles of stems and branches.

Wrens tend to concentrate their foraging efforts low down in the undergrowth, which is why they are cryptically coloured, to match the browns of leaf litter. Goldcrests focus on the overgrowth, which is why green colouration is a better camouflage. Both species also make their nests accordingly. The wren's nest is close to the ground and well hidden, in a cavity or between forked branches. The goldcrest's nest is similar to that of the long-tailed tit, comprising a hollow ball of moss and spider web held between small branches. However, they choose to build in conifer trees, because the needles provide a better matrix of support and greater concealment.

▲ The Troglodytes, from which the wren (*Troglodytes troglodytes*) derives its scientific name, are a mythological tribe of cave dwellers. The wren's habit of skulking in dark recesses clearly inspired the name.

◥ Due to its method of nest building, the goldcrest (*Regulus regulus*) favours conifer trees, but it will also use yew trees and hedges, as the yew has similar needle-shaped and evergreen foliage.

▶ Although the goldcrest and the firecrest (*Regulus ignicapillus*) are very similar in plumage, on closer inspection the firecrest has a distinct black line across the eye, with a white brow above.

Wrens will readily use nest boxes positioned in the right places, and they will also use them for roosting outside of the breeding season. Many wrens will cram into a single nest box to share their warmth in winter. Tits behave in a similar way, and will even stack up inside scaffold pipes in order to avoid wind and rain.

Passerines: Sparrows and dunnocks

Although its plumage is similarly coloured, with browns and greys, the dunnock is not from the same family as the sparrows. This is apparent by looking at the beak, which is slender and suited to eating invertebrates, while sparrows have beaks designed for a more cosmopolitan diet, including seeds and fruits. The dunnock also constructs a very neat cup-shaped nest in thicket, which is why it is sometimes known as the hedge sparrow.

The true sparrows are cavity nesters. In the wild they use holes and cleavages in trees and banks, but suitable voids in walls and buildings are often used, especially in the case of the house sparrow. Both the tree sparrow and the house sparrow will use nest boxes, and they like to nest in colonies. This makes them rather localised, so that sparrow populations may thrive in the gardens at one end of a street but be absent from the gardens at the other end.

▼ As the house sparrow (*Passer domesticus*) is a communal species, it spends a good deal of time communicating and quarrelling with its neighbours. The constant chirping is often part of the background noise in urban areas.

▲ The female tree sparrow (*Passer montanus*) looks like the male, while the female house sparrow is rather dull in comparison with the male. Both species can produce two or three broods in a single season.

▲ The barn swallow (*Hirundo rustica*) is seen in every part of the British archipelago, including the outlying smaller islands. For many people the sight of its elegant flight is a quintessential part of the British countryside.

▼ In France the house martin (*Delichon urbicum*) is known as the window swallow, due to its habit of nesting beneath the eves of houses, where it distracts the eye as it flies up and down past the windows.

▲ The dunnock (*Prunella modularis*) belongs to a family of birds called accentors and is the only British species. The female dunnock is polyandrous, meaning that she mates with more than one male, so that each brood has mixed parenting.

Sparrows are the birds from which the name *passerine* is derived, largely because they are typical perching birds, being small, brown and unspecialised. Birdwatchers often use the term 'usbb' as an abbreviation for 'unidentified small brown birds' when they catch a fleeting glimpse of a bird but are uncertain of the species because there are so many to choose from. However, these days it is less likely to be a sparrow, because they prefer the pleasingly less immaculate and slightly unkempt gardens and outhouses that the British used to have in the twentieth century, where they could find more food and nest sites. Numbers have declined as a natural adjustment to our overly tidy and manicured way of life in modern times.

Passerines: Swallows and martins

Passerines have evolved to exploit many of the available econiches in Britain. The flycatchers specialise in catching airborne insects, but they do so by launching sorties from favourite perches. The barn swallow, the house martin and the sand martin also specialise in hunting flying insects, but they do so by remaining on the wing for prolonged periods. As taking to the air requires effort, they optimise their efficiency by gathering insects in open airspace, leaving the flycatchers to exploit closed airspace.

Barn swallows are ledge nesters in the wild, but barns, stables, sties and sheds often offer ideal nesting sites on roof beams. They typically come and go through small openings, which they navigate in flight. Their nests are made from mud, reinforced with lengths of straw, feathers and other fibrous materials. While swallows nest *on* ledges, house martins nest *under* ledges. They have taken nest making to another level, by using pellets of mud to adhere their nests to sheltered surfaces that would otherwise have no attraction to birds. A scallop of pellets has further layers added, until a cup-shape is formed, which has geometric

▲ In the field, the sand martin (*Riparia riparia*) is told from the house martin by its lack of a white rump. As its scientific name implies, it is usually seen in riparian or riverside habitats, where it finds banks to excavate its nest tunnels.

▲ Despite its drab colouration, the spotted flycatcher (*Muscicapa striata*) is an elegant bird, as it perches with an upright posture to ensure that it has clear vision of passing prey insects all around and can sortie in any direction.

stability and strength. In the wild, house martins nest on rocky overhangs, but the eaves of houses have become a favoured place to build.

Sand martins are less common because they have a third method of nesting, by tunnelling into precipitous banks or cliffs of sandy substrate. In fact, before the introduction of human buildings into the landscape barn swallows and house martins would have been far less common too, because natural places to nest would have been relatively few and far between.

As swallows and martins have such a specialised diet, they cannot survive British winters, when flying insects are unavailable to hunt. For this reason they have to migrate southward to the African continent in order to find sufficient food. It is worth returning to Britain and Europe in the springtime, however, because the glut of seasonal insects allows them to breed. If they remained in Africa there would be no sudden abundance of food, because the seasonal emergence of insects becomes less pronounced towards the equator. Annual migration north and south is therefore a vital survival strategy, just as it is also for flycatchers and other insect-dependent birds.

Passerines: Flycatchers

As their name suggests, these birds are expert at hunting flies and other flying insects. While swallows and martins actively pursue their quarry in open areas, flycatchers employ a different strategy in woodland clearings and along forest margins. They sit on perches with favourable vantage points and wait for insects to fly past. They then dart off to take their prize and re-alight, on the same perch if it is nearest or another if that is nearer. By choosing busy insect flight paths they needn't waste very much time and effort in making their living, as long as the weather is dry enough for flying insects to be aloft. At other times they have to search for

insects and their larvae sheltering amidst the foliage of trees and shrubs.

Pied flycatchers are birds of deciduous woodland, so they only occur in rural gardens in appropriate habitat. Spotted flycatchers are far more widespread and better able to survive in urbanised habitat. While the pied flycatcher has striking black and white plumage, the spotted flycatcher is rather inconspicuous and easily overlooked because it is rather drab. However, it can be entertaining to watch as it performs aerobatics in pursuit of insects, over and over again.

Both species will use nest boxes. The pied flycatcher is a cavity nester and prefers a nest box with a hole, while the spotted flycatcher naturally nests on open ledges and in cleavages in trees, so it favours the open-fronted nest box.

▼ The male pied flycatcher (*Ficedula hypoleuca*) is a smart-looking bird in its two-tone plumage. The female has rather less contrasting colouration, in muted browns and creams rather than black and white.

▲ The male chaffinch (*Fringilla coelebs*) is one of Britain's most colourful birds, albeit hued in pastel shades. The chaffinch is also a common or garden species, seen in both rural and urban areas.

▲ The female chaffinch (*Fringilla coelebs*) has greenish plumage where the male's is reddish. This is to provide a better level of camouflage when the hen is incubating eggs on the nest.

Passerines: Finches and buntings

Taxonomically, finches and buntings belong to different scientific families, but they are so similar in appearance and habits that there would seem to be nothing to separate them. The finches belong to the *Fringillidae* and the buntings belong to the *Emberizidae*. The species from which these families get their name are the chaffinch and the yellowhammer respectively.

Finches and buntings are essentially seed-eating birds, although they will also eat insects and other invertebrates. Their beaks vary in size and shape from one species to another, according to the specific diets for which they are adapted. For example, some have tweezer-like beaks for teasing seeds from the heads of thistles, while others have more robust beaks for cracking the pits and stone of drupes, and a few have secateur-like beaks for dealing with pine-cone seeds. Most have more general beaks for handling the variety of seeds, fruits and invertebrates found in more general habitats, including most British gardens.

Male finches and buntings are typically more strikingly marked and coloured than females. The females often have rather more cryptic plumage to make them less conspicuous on the nest, which is typically built in dense thicket. Finches are rather neater in their nest-making and tend to place them on branches, while buntings tend to make their nests nearer to the ground in the undergrowth. Many finches are common or garden species, often seen on our lawns and bird tables, while buntings are seen in gardens rather less often, preferring more rural habitats.

◤ ▼ The male brambling (*Fringilla montifringilla*) looks rather like a badly painted male chaffinch. The female brambling is virtually identical to the female chaffinch, but with more mottled colouration.

▲ Although the siskin (*Carduelis spinus*) has a slender bill it is not designed for catching insects, as one might presume. In fact it is used for prizing the seeds from the small cones of spruce trees.

▼ Oddly, the plumage of the greenfinch (*Carduelis chloris*) becomes brighter as it wears, because the feathers fray slightly and reflect more light. The male's is particularly verdant, while the female is a rather duller green.

▲ The smallest British finch, the serin (*Serinus serinus*), has recently begun to extend its range from the Continent into southern England, which may be a response to climatic warming.

▼ The tweezer-like bill of the goldfinch (*Carduelis carduelis*) is an adaptation for teasing the seeds from thistle heads. The male and female are similar and look quite exotic with their red faces and yellow wing flashes.

▲▼◄► The linnet (*Carduelis cannabina*), the twite (*C. flavirostris*), the lesser redpoll (*C. cabaret*) and the common redpoll (*C. flammea*) are all rather similar finches. They all have brownish speckled body plumage, with varying amounts of reddish or pinkish colouring on the face and breast. It was only recently that the latter two were recognised as separate species, such is their likeness.

▼ The secateurs-like bill of the crossbill (*Loxia curvirostra*) has evolved to allow the bird to feed on pine nuts. The curvature in the bill enables the bird to lever open the bracts of pine cones and hook out the seeds with its tongue. There are two very similar species, the Scottish crossbill (*L. scotica*) and the parrot crossbill (*L. pytyopsittacus*), which it requires a knowledgeable eye to tell apart.

► Each of the finches is adapted to fill a slightly different econiche. The hawfinch (*Coccothraustes coccothraustes*) has a heavy-duty bill, equipped with robust muscles, for cracking open the stones of wild cherries and damsons to get at the kernels inside.

▶ Although the bill of the bullfinch (*Pyrrhula pyrrhula*) is relatively thickset, it is not particularly strong or tough. It is designed for nipping off tree buds and biting chunks out of firm fruits, such as crab apples and wild damsons. The female is identical to the male, but she is dusty pink instead of rose red, so that she is inconspicuous on the nest.

▲ The snow bunting (*Plectrophenax nivalis*) is more likely to be seen in gardens during the winter, when its plumage is dirty white and brown. In the breeding season the male has a pied plumage, in black and white.

▲ The yellowhammer (*Emberiza citrinella*) is found in nearly all of Britain, but it prefers open countryside. It does come to rural gardens in autumn and winter, however, when there is an opportunity to feed on seed.

▲ The cirl bunting (*Emberiza cirlus*) is now restricted to the south-west peninsula of England. It used to feed on the grain spill in stubble fields across southern England, but changes in farming practices have seen its numbers reduced.

▼ The corn bunting (*Emberiza calandra*) is often overlooked in rural gardens, because it looks very much like the female house sparrow, among which it will often feed as part of a mixed flock.

▼ During spring and summer, the reed bunting (*Emberiza schoeniclus*) frequents the environs of the reed beds where it nests, but during autumn and winter it will often visit rural gardens in search of food.

Passerines: Thrushes and starlings

We have only one member of the starling family, so called because its spangled plumage reminds the eye of the night sky filled with stars. It also has a glossy iridescent sheen in summer, making it quite exotic-looking at close quarters.

The starling is a worm-feeding specialist, which is why it is often seen on expanses of lawn in gardens, parks and school grounds. Its technique is to patter the ground with its feet in imitation of rain, so that earthworms are drawn to the surface to feed, because they need moisture to lubricate the soil. The starling then repeatedly probes the ground with its beak open, so that it is able to quickly close its beak on a worm and pull it from the soil before it has a chance to retract. Flocks of starlings often work together, so that their combined footfalls bring many worms within reach.

Starlings are hole-nesters and they live in loose colonies. The eaves of houses near to suitable areas for feeding are favoured in the urban environment, although in rural areas they will use cavities in trees and feed in fields grazed by livestock, where they find many other invertebrates to eat in association with dung. With the advent of plastic fascias and soffits, starlings have found it increasingly difficult to find nesting sites in the roofs of houses and have therefore declined in numbers. They will readily use nest boxes instead, especially if a number of similar boxes are in near proximity.

In contrast to our lone starling, many members of the thrush family can be seen in British gardens. They are grouped into small thrushes and large thrushes. The small thrushes include the robin, the nightingale and the redstart, while the large thrushes include the blackbird, the song thrush and the mistle thrush. They are all essentially woodland species that divide their time between the ground and the tress, where they hunt for a wide variety of invertebrates, including insects, spiders, worms and snails.

As a number of thrush species may be found in the same habitat, it follows that they tend to occupy slightly different econiches to avoid direct competition for resources. Their relative size is an indication of this, as they naturally frequent parts of habitat where they are a good physical match to the available gaps between obstacles. Smaller species can therefore fit into tighter spaces and exploit resources that the larger species cannot reach.

A good deal of their food is found by turning leaf litter and detritus, under which many small animals are living and hiding. This is why robins have the habit of following gardeners as they dig the top soil, as the birds are making the most of a feeding opportunity without expending much effort. Also, by being bold they get to pick off the morsels of food before other thrush species get a chance to investigate the newly turned ground.

The thrush family typically build cup-shaped nests in thicket or in natural recesses in the wild. They will also use cavities in old walls and ledges in outbuildings. Open-fronted nest boxes are readily commandeered by many species, while redstarts will also use hole-fronted nest boxes.

The term 'songbird' is exemplified by the thrushes, as they are renowned for their elaborate vocal choruses. The nightingale is the most celebrated of them all, but other species are just as pleasing to the ear. This characteristic is a clue as to the woodland habitat in which these birds evolved, and which once covered most of Britain. In an environment where visibility is restricted by foliage, having a pronounced and intricate song is useful for attracting mates and deterring competitors from territories. The males can be heard exercising their voice boxes at dawn and at dusk, when they are not busy foraging.

Humans have a voice box called a larynx, which works by passing a stream of air between vocal chords. Birds have a voice box called a syrinx, which works in a different way. A series of rings around the trachea allow the windpipe to change shape rapidly and with great variation, so that songbirds can issue such complex and tuneful songs. In contrast to these bird *songs*, birds also make *calls*, which are more prosaic sounds used for general communication. For example, there are contact calls, so that birds can locate one another, and there are alarm calls, so that birds can warn each other about the presence of predators.

▲▼ The blackbird (*Turdus merula*) is one of Britain's most familiar garden birds, equally at home in our towns and cities as it is in our villages and hamlets. It is a highly adaptable all-rounder, in terms of diet, behaviour and size.

▲◥ The song thrush (*Turdus philomelos*) has carved an econiche for itself by exploiting the abundance of snails found in British gardens. It uses a stone as an anvil, against which it smashes their shells to extract the gastropod flesh.

▶ A larger and more elegant bird than the song thrush, the mistle thrush (*Turdus viscivorus*) favours gardens and parks with open lawns and mature trees. In the field it can be identified by the larger, overlapping spots on its breast, with a paler ground colour.

▼ The fieldfare (*Turdus pilaris*) is a winter visitor to Britain from its breeding grounds further north in Scandinavia. Berries are an important source of food and it will migrate considerable distances until it finds them.

◢ In flight the redwing (*Turdus iliacus*) exposes the flashes of rusty-red on its underwings from which it gets its name. Like the fieldfare, it is a winter visitor and the two species can often be seen travelling together in large flocks.

▲ The robin (*Erithacus rubecula*) was once though to be the cock bird to the wren, because in both species the male and female are identical. Thus they were called robin redbreast and jenny wren.

▲ The juvenile robin has cryptic plumage, much like the fledglings of other members of the thrush family. This enables them to hide in the thicket while their parents continue to feed them, until they learn to fend for themselves.

◀ As well as having an intricate song, the nightingale (*Luscinia megarhynchos*) also has a rather loud voice, so that it carries across the woodland in which it lives. When seen in the flesh, the nightingale is a surprisingly lacklustre bird.

◣▼ So called because the red starts in its tail, the male redstart (*Phoenicurus phoenicurus*) is a splendid-looking bird. The female redstart is dressed down in comparison, so that she is not noticed by predators.

▲ The name of the stonechat (*Saxicola rubetra*) alludes to its call, which sounds similar to a pair of pebbles glancing, or chatting, against one another. This bird lives in areas of scrubland and heathland, where plenty of insects are available.

▶ The wheatear (*Oenarthe oenarthe*) was once eaten as a delicacy in Britain. Shepherds would supplement their incomes by trapping the birds and selling them alive to poulterers, who would deliver them to the fashionable gentry.

▼ The starling (*Sturnus vulgaris*) has probably seen a more dramatic decline in numbers than any other British bird. Fewer nesting sites and changes in farming practices have conspired to reduce the starling's ability to reproduce.

▲ The word 'whin' is another name for gorse, as the whinchat (*Saxicola rubetra*) is found in heathland, where gorse bushes grow and where the bird makes its nest. The whinchat is a summer visitor, while the stonechat is a British resident.

▼ The numbers of waxwings (*Bombycilla garrulous*) visiting British gardens in the winter months varies each year. It depends on their breeding success in Scandinavia, as greater numbers of waxwings require greater quantities of berries.

Passerines: Wagtails and warblers

These two families of birds are insectivorous, which is why they have delicate beaks. While flycatchers, swallows and martins specialise in catching airborne insects in clearings and open skies, the wagtails and warblers hunt flying insects closer to the ground, above water or in amongst foliage, where they also pick them off leaves and other surfaces, along with larvae and other invertebrates.

Wagtails are so called because they have a habit of wagging their long tails up and down. Although this habit would appear to make them more conspicuous to predators, it actually helps them to evade predation by mimicking the movements of wind-blown plants. Predators instinctively look for movement in a particular direction, so this habitual movement back and forth causes predators to ignore what they see.

Warblers get their name from their song, which has a rapid oscillating quality, otherwise known as a warble. Each species has its own characteristic pattern and tone of song and call. This makes it possible to identify different warblers even when they are nowhere to be seen, hidden in the undergrowth and thicket. In fact, warblers can be quite difficult to separate visually because they are typically rather drab and indistinct in appearance. In essence they have evolved to be invisible as they skulk amongst the sward, herbage and greenery in which they live.

▶ The grey wagtail (*Motacilla cinerea*) favours habitat where it can hunt flying insects with aquatic larvae, so it is found in the environs of rivers, streams, lakes and ponds.

▼ Unlike the pied and grey wagtails, the yellow wagtail (*Motacilla flava*) is only in Britain during the breeding season. Its Latin scientific name means yellow (*flava*) tail (*cilla*) mover (*mota*).

▲ The pied wagtail (*Motacilla alba*) is commonly seen in both urban and rural settings, where it hunts for insects on open flat areas, such as driveways, roofs, lawns, sports pitches and tennis courts.

▼ The grasshopper warbler (*Locustella naevia*) is so called because it has a call that sounds very much like a stridulating grasshopper. It is more often heard than seen, as it tends to skulk in deep undergrowth.

▲ The reed warbler (*Acrocephalus scirpaceus*) prefers to nest in reed beds, due to the way it constructs its nest and the availability of insects, but it will also nest in stands of willowherb and cereal crop.

▲ Juvenile sedge warblers (*Acrocephalus schoenobaenus*) have an interesting behaviour. When they sense danger they point their heads skyward, so that their cryptic camouflage is even more effective against the plant stems.

▲ Although very similar to the common whitethroat, the lesser whitethroat (*Sylvia curruca*) has greyish wings, while the other bird has chestnut wings. The lesser whitethroat is also more likely to be seen in gardens.

▲ The male whitethroat (*Sylvia communis*) defers to the discernment of the female in choice of nest site. He does so by building a number of starter nests – known as cock nests – so that she can choose one for completion.

◀▶ Only the male blackcap (*Sylvia atricapilla*) has the diagnostic black crown to its head, while the crown of the female is a chestnut brown colour. It is often seen in gardens, weaving its way through the undergrowth in search of insects.

▲ The garden warbler (*Sylvia borin*) looks much the same as the blackcap, but without the black or chestnut crown. It is attracted to unkempt gardens, with plenty of bramble growth, where it can nest safe from predators.

▼ ◣▶ It is fair to say the chiffchaff (*Phylloscopus collybita*), the willow warbler (*P. trochilus*) and the wood warbler (*P. sibilatrix*) might easily be confused with one another in the field. A tip is to look for the saturation of yellow and green in the plumage. The wood warbler is relatively brightly coloured, while the chiffchaff is quite dull, and the willow warbler falls somewhere in between.

Passerines: Larks and pipits

These species are possibly the least conspicuous among garden birds, as they have cryptic plumage and they spend most of their time hidden in tall grasses and undergrowth along the margins between meadow and hedgerow or woodland. They build their nests at ground level and hunt for a wide variety of small insects and other invertebrates. The males of both larks and pipits have song flights, which they use to attract females and to establish their territories. The species sometimes seen in gardens are the tree pipit and the woodlark, as these are adapted to life in the kind of habitat that gardens can offer. They are unlikely to nest in gardens as they are easily predated by domestic cats.

◥▶ The woodlark (*Lullula arborea*) and the skylark (*Alauda arvensis*) both have the habit of singing whilst ascending skyward, and then descending back to terra firma. The woodlark prefers countryside with trees and scrub, so may be seen in some rural gardens. The skylark likes its habitat to be more open. Both species have crests, but the skylark's is more pronounced.

▼◢ The tree pipit (*Anthus trivialis*) and the meadow pipit (*A. pratensis*) are very similar in appearance. Without intimate knowledge of their different calls and songs, the best way to distinguish them is by habitat. As their common names suggest, one prefers woodland while the other prefers grassland. The tree pipit is a migrant species, while the meadow pipit is resident.

Passerines: cuckoo

Perhaps the most notorious passerine is the cuckoo, because it has evolved to parasitise other songbirds. It takes advantage of the parental instincts in other nesting birds, which are duped into rearing cuckoo chicks as their own. The female cuckoo invests a great deal of time and effort into locating the nests of several pairs of potential host birds. At the right moment, she then supplants one of their eggs with her own in each nest. Cuckoos look similar to sparrowhawks, so the hosts evacuate the area to avoid predation while the deception is made. Although the cuckoo's egg is larger, it is marked and coloured to mimic those of the hosts, so they happily incubate it. The cuckoo hatchling then ejects the other eggs or chicks from the nest and takes all of the food brought by its surrogate parents. It even imitates the call of several offspring to prompt the host birds to bring increasing numbers of insects to satisfy its appetite.

As the female cuckoo evidently has to work quite hard anyway to achieve reproductive success, it is not immediately apparent how the strategy brings benefits, when she might as well rear her own offspring. The answer lies in the numbers of cuckoo chicks nurtured to adulthood, as the strategy effectively means that the cuckoo is simultaneously multi-brooding. As cuckoos are migratory, this means that the breeding season is too short for a larger bird to multi-brood in the conventional way, so parasitising other birds is a means of doing so.

Cuckoos have their own econiche in woodland habitats, as they specialise in eating hairy caterpillars, which other birds avoid because the hairs are defensively armed with irritants. They have been able to specialise in this way because they have no need to feed their young with the same food, which would be hazardous to a developing chick. The caterpillars are bashed against branches to kill them and gut them. This makes the hairs lie flat so that the caterpillars can then be swallowed head-first without harm to the cuckoo's gullet.

▲ The male cuckoo (*Cuculus canorus*) declares his arrival in Britain to any nearby females from a high perch, where he issues the diagnostic *cuckoo* call. The call carries well over distance so that mates can be found.

▼ Reed warblers are often chosen as hosts by cuckoos, probably because their nests are relatively easy to access by the much larger parasitic bird. The warblers instinctively feed the chick even though it dwarfs them.

◀▲▲▼ In flight, and whilst perching, the cuckoo shows remarkably similar outline, posture, markings and colouring to the sparrowhawk. It even has eyes with yellow irises as well as yellow legs and feet. As all small birds are terrified of sparrowhawks, this mimicry serves very well in temporarily scaring the host birds away, so that they don't see the female cuckoo switching eggs in their nest.

Picidae: Woodpeckers

Woodpeckers typically excavate their nest holes from old timber in standing dead trees or from rotten patches in living trees. They prefer to tunnel into soft decaying wood because it is far easier to chisel away, thus avoiding excessive effort and possible injury. Many other birds commandeer old woodpecker nest holes too, so these birds perform an important ecological function by increasing the number of potential nest sites in woodland habitat. Woodpeckers also rely on standing and fallen dead trees to find their food, which comprises the larvae of wood-boring beetles and moths. They puncture the surface of the wood to find the insects and then use a barbed tongue to hook them out.

The greater spotted woodpecker and lesser spotted woodpecker are similar in appearance, but there is a considerable size difference, the former being about the size of a mistle thrush and the latter the size of a robin. This belies their adaptation to slightly different econiches within the same habitat. The greater spotted woodpecker nests in and feeds on the trunks and large limbs of mature trees, while the lesser spotted woodpecker exploits the smaller limbs and branches of mature trees. Both species can therefore co-exist without direct competition for resources.

The green woodpecker is larger still than the greater spotted woodpecker and is partly terrestrial in its habits. It will often search for worms and insect larvae in meadows and lawns, which is why it is green in colour. This affords it some camouflage from aerial predators such as buzzards, goshawks and large falcons while it forages in the open. Green woodpeckers also like to spend time *anting* themselves – they spread their wings over the nests of wood ants and encourage the insects to attack, which they do by spraying formic acid. The acid effectively dry-cleans the birds' plumage by ridding their feathers of parasitic lice, mites and fleas. Other birds do a similar thing by dust bathing and, of course, bathing in water.

Woodpeckers will use nest boxes on occasion. They prefer to have boxes filled with material they can excavate, such as blocks of polyurethane foam or expanded polystyrene, or stacks of corrugated cardboard or balsa sheets. That way, they can fashion the shape of the interior as they would naturally in a tree cavity. This is important in allowing the chicks to reach the entrance to be fed, by bracing the sides with their feet. A woodpecker box therefore needs to be an appropriate size to accommodate the volume of surrounding material required.

▼ The green woodpecker (*Picus viridis*) used to be known as the *yaffle*, due to its call, which sounds something like a comedic human laugh. The adults predigest food and then regurgitate it to feed their young.

▼ A medium-sized species, the great spotted woodpecker (*Dendrocopos major*) is a frequent visitor to many gardens, especially in winter, when it alights on bird tables and feeders.

▼ For a woodpecker, the lesser spotted (*Dendrocopos minor*) is remarkably small, being only slightly larger than a finch or sparrow. It can easily be overlooked as it works its way through the canopy in search of food.

Apodidae: Swifts

Despite their apparent similarity in form and lifestyle to swallows and martins, swifts are not closely related to them. In fact, the swift's closest relatives are the hummingbirds of the New World. Like hummingbirds, the swift has freely articulating shoulder joints, which allow it to both propel and steer itself with its wings, so that the tail is largely redundant in flight. This is why the swift appears to be flapping its wings independent of one another, as it uses a different flying technique to all other British birds.

The swift specialises in catching airborne insects and is so well adapted to life in the air that it seldom lands. It has very short legs suited for alighting on elevated perches on cliff faces and large trees, where it can relaunch itself simply by dropping. When swifts find themselves accidentally grounded they struggle to take to the air, as they find it difficult to flap their wings free of the ground to create the necessary lift. They require level ground and sufficient space as a runway. Only a few failed take-off attempts tires them out too much to succeed.

In a wild setting, swifts nest on ledges on precipices and in caves, but they have taken to nesting in the roofs of buildings. They enter between loose tiles or behind fascias and soffits and create very rudimentary nests of debris on flat surfaces within. Some buildings have swift holes deliberately set in the tiles, with nesting shelves positioned behind. They nest in tall buildings to avoid the possibility of coming to earth as far as possible, because stranding is likely to end in death.

▲ The swift (*Apus apus*) is so well adapted to flight that it even copulates on the wing. When hunting it collects insects in its mouth until a bolus is formed, so that it doesn't waste time and energy visiting the nest more often than it needs to.

Strigiformes: Owls

There are three owls that may be seen in gardens, depending on the part of Britain. The most widespread and common is the tawny owl, which is the quintessential 'wise owl' of children's stories, both in terms of appearance and call, which is the classic *twit-twoo*. It is commonly thought that the female owl calls *twit*, and the male responds with *twoo*, but in fact both sexes can make the whole call. It is true, however, that males and females make overlapping calls to communicate in the dark, so sometimes they both contribute to the whole call.

Tawny owls are common in town and country, because their food is usually plentiful. They eat small terrestrial mammals (rodents and shrews) and small passerine birds (finches, tits, warblers etc), which they swallow whole. As

▶ The typical roost and nest site of the tawny owl (*Strix aluco*) is a rotted cavity where a large limb has broken away from a mature tree. They often go unnoticed in urban gardens and parks as they are so well camouflaged.

▲ The little owl (*Athene noctua*) was introduced to Britain from Continental Europe in the 19th century. It has established itself because it doesn't compete with other owls, as it prefers smaller prey, such as worms, crickets and beetles.

▼ Just as the tawny owl is adapted for woodland, so the barn owl (*Tyto alba*) is adapted for meadows. It is relatively less common as a result, because hay meadows and other types of grassland are fewer and far between.

long as there are mature trees available in which to nest and roost then tawny owls will include a number of gardens in their territories. They usually nest in hollows in trees, but they will also nest at the junction of large tree limbs and in the old nests of large birds. Nest boxes are often used too, which are designed to imitate tree cavities.

Barn owls and little owls are birds of more rural areas, because their hunting habits are more specific. Barn owls specialise in catching small mammals in meadows by silently patrolling above the sward until they hear movements, and then dropping down on to their prey. Little owls specialise in eating large invertebrates, such as worms and beetles, but will also take small mammals and birds. Both will use nest boxes of appropriate size and design. The tawny owl and barn owl are both nocturnal, while the little owl is diurnal, meaning it is active by day.

Owls are unusual among birds in having asymmetric ears – they are positioned slightly differently on each side of the head. This enables them to more accurately pinpoint the position of prey, because their brains are able to measure the minuscule differences in the time that sound waves arrive in each ear; they take a bearing up and down, as well as left and right, so that a cross marks the spot. They also have stereoscopic vision, just like humans, which means they can see in three dimensions and judge depth and distance very well.

▲◥▶ The grey heron (*Ardea cinerea*) is a surprisingly large and rather primeval-looking bird. Compared with other large water birds, such as swans and geese, the grey heron requires very little space to become airborne, which is an adaptation to fishing and nesting in trees. Its large wings enable it to take off almost vertically, and its neck is folded so that its head is kept away from obstacles as it ascends.

Ardeide: Herons

Scolopacidae: Sandpipers

These are all long-legged and long-billed birds that make their living from feeding on freshwater vertebrates and invertebrates. Herons will visit ponds in surprisingly small gardens, because hunting is so easy. Many pond fish are highly visible, and they are also contained within a small volume of water so that herons have no problem catching them. In wild habitats, herons need to invest far more time and effort into hunting on the edges of lakes and rivers, so garden ponds are like fast-food buffets for them.

Grey herons nest communally in large trees in riparian and marshy places, but they travel considerable distances to raid garden ponds, so they may be nesting several miles away. They have large wings adapted for efficient flight over long distances, and they are large birds to enable them to catch large fish at depth and to carry the weight back to the nest. Herons can therefore exploit urban ponds yet nest and roost out in the green belt. In effect, they commute to work.

In marked contrast to the grey heron, the other garden waders are far smaller and feed by probing their bills into mud and damp substrate, which is why they are collectively known as sandpipers. The redshank and snipe are sometimes seen in gardens with large shallow bodies of water where they can both feed and breed. The woodcock is less reliant on water, as it is adapted for life on forest floors, although it does like drainage ditches and waterlogged clearings where the humus and soil is soft enough to probe for worms. All three species are cryptically coloured as they are ground nesters and camouflage is essential for concealment from predators.

◀ As an example of cryptic camouflage, the woodcock (*Scolopax rusticola*) is hard to beat. It sits on the woodland floor among dead leaves during the day, where it blends with the background

▼ The snipe (*Gallinago gallinago*) is smaller and slimmer compared with the woodcock, and it has a proportionately long bill. The tip of the bill is flexible in both species, so that worms can be grasped while the bill is immersed in mud.

▲ The ring-necked pheasant (*Phasianus colchicus*) is so called because it often has a white collar. There are many plumage variations in the male, but the female tends to be uniformly cryptic in pattern and colouration.

▼ Despite its name, the grey partridge (*Perdix perdix*) is actually quite colourful and striking close up. The dark patch on the breast varies in shape and size between individuals. It is usually more horseshoe-shaped.

▲ The red-legged partridge (*Alectoris rufa*) was introduced to Britain in the late 18th century from French stock. It is a slighter larger and stockier bird than the native grey partridge, and it is more reluctant to fly.

Phasianidae: Gamebirds
Rallidae: Gallinules

These birds are plump-bodied, with fairly long legs and medium-sized bills. Gamebirds are adapted for life on dry land, while gallinules are adapted for a semi-aquatic lifestyle. They are fundamentally vegetarian in diet, but also eat a wide variety of insects and other invertebrates.

The three gamebirds most likely to be seen in British gardens are the ring-necked pheasant, the common partridge and the red-legged partridge. Pheasants are often quite bold, because they have been reared by gamekeepers to provide quarry for those who find sport in shooting animals, but partridges are generally far more timid and less often seen in the open. As gamebirds are not strong fliers, they are reluctant to take to the air unless absolutely necessary. They typically crouch in the undergrowth when humans and predators come near and will suddenly burst upwards on the wing if the perceived danger gets too close. In the wild they feed primarily on seeds and other plant matter, so grain and legume crops are an attractive draw. Gamebirds are most often seen in gardens near to areas of natural habitat.

Our gallinules are the coot and the moorhen. Both are quite common on and around large ponds, lakes and slow-flowing streams and rivers. Moorhens in particular will make use of large garden ponds, as they are the smaller of the two species. Like gamebirds, they too are disinclined to become airborne, and are far more likely to run and hide amongst the vegetation or to scramble to open water if danger threatens. They nest on islands of water plants, where terrestrial predators find it difficult to reach them.

Gamebirds and gallinules have precocial chicks, which means that they are able to leave the nest soon after hatching, so that the parents can lead them to food and away from danger.

▲ The familiarity of the white forehead of the coot (*Fulica atra*) has given rise to the expression 'as bald as a coot'. Its purpose is to act as a protective shield when the bird feeds by grabbing water weed from the bottom of ponds.

▲ The moorhen (*Gallinula chloropus*) is more likely to frequent garden ponds than the coot, because it is a smaller bird. Despite its hen-like shape, the moorhen is not closely related to chickens.

Anatidae: Waterfowl, grebes and kingfishers

The mallard duck, Canada goose and mute swan are the three species of waterfowl encountered most frequently in British gardens with sizeable ponds. They are equally at home in rural and urban habitats, as they have catholic diets, eating water weeds, invertebrates and the scraps of bread that the British love to feed them. They sometimes nest in the most unlikely places and then march their hatchlings to water by negotiating roads and other man-made obstacles. Urban populations often do very well, because people are inclined to feed and protect them, and they have fewer natural predators.

▼▶The mallard (*Anas platyrhynchos*) is so commonplace on ponds in gardens and parks that we often forget that it is a wild species too. Both sexes have iridescent blue wing flashes, which are seen in flight.

◀▲ Wild ducks, such as the teal (*Anas crecca*), tend to be very wary in rural areas, because they are hunted for sport, but in urban areas they have learnt to be less fearful of humans.

◀▲ The tufted duck (*Aythya fuligula*) is a species that has taken advantage of human activity. Reservoirs and flooded quarries have allowed it to extend its range, so that it is now seen in urban areas.

▲▶ The pochard (*Aythya ferina*) and the tufted duck are diving ducks, as they feed by diving. The mallard and teal are dabbling ducks, as they cannot dive; instead they upend and feed at or near the surface of the water.

▲ The mute swan (*Cygnus olor*) is so named because it seldom calls, unlike other swans which can be remarkably noisy. Aesthetically the mute swan is very appealing to the human eye, because it is elegantly proportioned and pristine in colour.

▲ As its name suggests, the Canada goose (*Branta canadensis*) was introduced to Britain from North America. Like the mallard duck and the white swan, it is given to tameness and has become a common site in public gardens and parks.

▼ For its size, the kingfisher (*Alcedo atthis*) packs a remarkable visual punch. It is usually seen darting along the sides of rivers and lakes, with a flash of iridescent blue as its back plumage catches the sunlight.

▲ Like all grebes, the little grebe (*Tachybaptus ruficollis*) is ungainly on land, because its legs are positioned to the rear of the body as an adaptation to diving for fish, amphibians and aquatic invertebrates.

▼ Seen here with a perch in its bill, the great crested grebe (*Podiceps cristatus*) is twice the size of the little grebe, and is therefore seen on larger ponds and lakes where suitable prey is available.

◀▼ The herring gull (*Larus argentatus*), the lesser black-backed gull (*L. fuscus*) and the great black-backed gull (*L. marinus*) are all large gulls with yellow bills. The red spots on their bills are pecked by their chicks to stimulate regurgitation of food. The herring gull has a silver-grey back and pink feet, the lesser black-backed gull has a gunmetal-grey back and yellow feet, and the greater black-backed gull has a charcoal-grey back and pink feet. There is also a slight increase in their sizes respectively.

Sternidae: Gulls and cormorants

Gulls are increasingly seen in and around garden habitats, because their populations are adapting to inland environments. They nest on the flat roofs of urban buildings, because these imitate the coastal cliff ledges upon which they would naturally reproduce. There is also plenty of food available. Landfill sites offer a bounty of waste food, our streets are frequently strewn with fast-food leftovers and our lawns are often scattered with scraps. It is remarkable how quickly gulls will begin wheeling above a garden when food is thrown out. It is also remarkable how rapidly the food is consumed, as gulls are able to swallow very large morsels of food. In the wild they are scavengers and opportunists, capable of gulping whole chicks and fish down their throats, which is a useful adaptation for urban living.

The larger gull species most often seen are the herring gull and the lesser black-backed gull, as they are the species that utilise town and city rooftops. The smaller common gull and black-headed gull are also seen taking food in gardens, but they are less inclined to nest on buildings and usually breed in colonies on the edges of large bodies of water, such as reservoirs and lakes. Gulls are intelligent and resourceful birds and have been known to use morsels of bread as bait to catch fish from ponds.

◀▶ The black-headed gull (*Chroicocephalus ridibundus*) only has its black head during the breeding season. During the winter it has a small black smudge behind each eye.

▶ The cormorant (*Phalacrocorax carbo*) is really a bird of coast and estuary, but it has begun to frequent inland rivers, lakes, ponds and reservoirs. It is clearly equally at home fishing in saltwater, brackish water and freshwater.

▼ The common gull (*Larus canus*) is similar in appearance to the herring gull. On closer inspection, however, it has yellow feet and is about two-thirds the size. It also lacks the red spot on the bill.

▲ The collared dove (*Streptopelia decaocto*) introduced itself to Britain in the 1950s and has since colonised every part of the archipelago. It is often a notably tame bird, quite happy to nest close to human activity.

▲ As the collared dove has become commonplace in Britain, so its close relative the turtle dove (*Streptopelia turtur*) has become increasingly uncommon. Unlike the collared dove it is a migrant species and this may be a factor.

▼ Larger than the other doves, the wood pigeon (*Columba palumbus*) is popular as a source of game meat. Despite its being shot in large numbers, the wood pigeon is very successful at replenishing its population.

▼ The stock dove (*Columba oenas*) is often overlooked amidst flocks alongside wood pigeons, but it is smaller and lacks the white patches on either side of the neck. It has incomplete black bars on its wings.

Columbidae: Doves (collared dove, turtle dove, wood pigeon, stock dove)

Doves and pigeons are essentially vegetarian, although they will supplement their diet with invertebrates when they get the chance. Their main foods are buds, shoots, leaves, berries, pulses and seeds. As these foods require processing to acquire sufficient nutrition, they are equipped with a crop and a gizzard. The crop is used to store large quantities of food prior to digestion. The food then travels to the first stomach, where digestive juices are added. Following this, it travels to the gizzard, which is a muscular stomach where the food it churned and broken down.

Young doves and pigeons are unable to digest the same food as their parents, so evolution has found a solution in the form of 'crop milk'. This is an edible substance secreted from the crop lining of the adults. It means that the birds can eat a wide variety of plant material, but still feed their offspring. Pigeons and doves are also able to drink water quickly by sucking, while other birds have to tip their heads back with a beak-full at a time. They need to drink a lot to aid in the digestion of their food, so the ability to drink rapidly is useful in avoiding predators while they are compromised.

Pigeons and doves construct rather messy looking nests from twigs, which look as if they might easily fall apart. They naturally choose forks in the canopy, ledges created by larger tree bows and large cavities but will also nest on open ledges of buildings. They typically have two offspring, which are often male and female, resulting in the phrase 'pigeon pair' when referring to boy-and-girl twins.

The terms *pigeon* and *dove* are interchangeable and are a vestige of Britain's turbulent past. Dove is derived from the Norse word *dúfa*, while pigeon is derived from the Norman word *pijon*. The birds have long been prized for their flesh and were originally domesticated as a reliable source of meat.

Corvidae: Crows (carrion crow, magpie, jay, rook, jackdaw)

Members of the crow family are generally regarded with disdain because they are large opportunists and predators, capable of causing havoc in gardens. They will bully other birds away from food, steal eggs from nests and even prey on nestlings. Of course, this is all quite natural behaviour, which explains their success, but it can appear to upset the ecological equilibrium, because we forget that our gardens are part of an extended habitat and environment in which the overall ecological balance takes care of itself.

The crow family is renowned for comprising the most intelligent of garden birds. It is this intelligence that makes them very adaptable and able to live alongside humans, where they exploit a wide variety of food sources. They are also very aggressive and competitive with one another, even when from the same species, so that noisy quarrels often break out. Most species are canopy nesters, but the smaller jackdaws nest in cavities. They are very inventive when it comes to nest sites and will often use chimney pots by blocking them with sticks. They will readily take to nest boxes too, as they live communally, so places to build are always at a premium.

▲ The wild rock dove (*Columba livia*) frequents coastal areas with cliff ledges for nesting. Feral or town pigeons are descended from the rock dove, and they do well in urban areas because they treat buildings as cliff ledges.

▲▼ The carrion crow (*Corvus corone*) and the hooded crow (*Corvus cornix*) used to be considered subspecies, but they now have separate species status. There is a clear line between the ranges of the two crows, so that the hooded crow occupies Ireland and western Scotland, while the carrion crow inhabits eastern Scotland, England and Wales. Hybrid birds occur along the boundary, but the two populations remain distinct.

▲ As the rook (*Corvus frugilegus*) has a naked face and a long pointed bill, it is likely that it evolved to scavenge viscera from large animal carcasses in the extensive areas of woodland that once covered Britain and the rest of Europe.

▲ With its contrasting pied plumage and long tail, the magpie (*Pica pica*) is an unmistakable British bird. When nesting it is very territorial, especially towards other members of the crow family and potential predators.

▼ The jackdaw (*Corvus monedula*) is smaller than the crow, magpie and jay, enabling it to nest in cavities. Juvenile jackdaws are readily tamed and make mischievous pets with a predilection for stealing shiny objects.

▼ The jay (*Garrulus glandarius*) looks quite exotic compared with the other members of the crow family, especially with its blue wing flashes. It is a bird of mixed woodland and large gardens.

Raptors: Buzzards, kestrels and sparrowhawks

In Britain there are three raptors that might be regarded as common or garden birds. They are the buzzard, the sparrowhawk and the kestrel. They don't often nest in gardens, because they require mature tree canopies, but they have large hunting territories that often include many gardens.

They each specialise in different prey groups, therefore avoiding direct competition with one another, and can often be seen in the same habitats. Kestrels specialise in hunting small mammals, such as mice and voles, which they spot from above by patrolling the skies. They are unique among birds of prey in their ability to hover, so that they are more effective at spotting the movements of their prey. Buzzards hunt larger animals, such as squirrels, rats, rabbits and grass snakes. They also hunt from the skies, by soaring on thermals and using very acute eyesight to spot their quarry. Sparrowhawks are expert at hunting small passerine birds. They ambush their prey by approaching stealthily through gaps in undergrowth and foliage.

By and large, therefore, these three raptors cover all of the available hunting econiches in British gardens, except for the nocturnal – which is why tawny owls also do so well, as they prey on the rodents and shrews that emerge after dark, as well as any roosting garden birds small enough to swallow whole.

Raptors tend to build their nests high in the forks of branches and on bows in large trees. However, sparrowhawks and kestrels will use nest boxes in places where hunting is good but natural nesting sites are difficult to find. Nest boxes need to be suitably large and sufficiently elevated and orientated, so that they appeal to the instincts that the birds use in choosing natural places to rear their young.

▼◢ The fortunes of the red kite (*Milvus milvus*) have improved over recent decades, so it has extended its range and become quite common in some areas. Many people leave carcass scraps in their gardens to attract the birds.

▲▼ The buzzard (*Buteo buteo*) is usually seen soaring at altitude, on the lookout for likely places to hunt. It will then patiently sit at a suitable vantage point, ready to launch an attack on an unsuspecting mammal or reptile.

▲▶ The kestrel (*Falco tinnunculus*) is able to hover in places where there are no available perches for hunting. This gives it the advantage of being able to patrol large areas of grassland and meadow, including road verges.

◀▼ Like the buzzard, the sparrowhawk (*Accipiter nisus*) will soar high to look for hunting opportunities and then descend to a location where it can ambush prey and make a successful kill.

Wildlife navigation

Bats are well known for their ability to navigate in darkness with echolocation, which means that they sense the location of obstacles and prey by listening for echoes. In effect, bats are so good at echolocation that they use their ears as eyes, so that the brain creates a mental image of its surroundings based on sound waves instead of light waves. Other animals navigate their way in their environments by using different sensual ways of seeing their surroundings.

Let us consider other senses that animals may use, aside from sight and hearing. A number of animals use touch as their primary means of navigation. For example, harvestmen use their elongated legs to feel their way through undergrowth. Centipedes, millipedes, woodlice and many insects use their antennae in a similar way, which is why they are often known as 'feelers'.

Many insects also navigate by sense of smell and taste, to locate sources of food and to find mates. For example, blowflies will follow the smell of decay and then use their feet to taste the putrefying carcass. Male moths follow scent trails to find females, and female moths taste food plants with their feet before laying their eggs.

Although we see things in white light, many insects use other parts of the light spectrum to see their surroundings. Nectar-feeding insects, such as butterflies, locate flowers by detecting the ultraviolet light they reflect. Similarly, some parasites use infrared light to locate hosts by their warmth.

Of course, most animals actually use a combination of senses to navigate in their environments. There are additional senses that also allow animals to coordinate themselves properly, such as a sense of balance and a kinaesthetic sense, which is knowing where different parts of the body are in relation to one another. As many birds and insects also steer their way over long distances on migration, it is also true that they are able to navigate by using landmarks and skymarks. This may also involve internal compasses, which guide them in relation to the position of magnetic north.

Wildlife ID and photography

Knowing the 'jizz'

The term 'jizz' is used by naturalists to describe the quintessential behavioural traits and fleeting appearances of animal species in the wild. The idea is that it becomes possible to surmise the identity of a species in motion based on its movements, its shape, its colouring and other information such as noises. There may also be physical evidence such as footprints and excreta – sometimes known as 'sign'. As many wild animals are only glimpsed briefly in passing, or from a distance, knowing their jizz can be very helpful for identification purposes.

Generally speaking, naturalists typically refer to 'the jizz' when referring to flying animals – birds, bats, butterflies, moths, dragonflies, damselflies, bees, wasps and other flying insects. For example, the size and silhouette of a bird, along with its pattern of flight, will go a long way to betraying the species or at least the family to which it belongs. Similarly, experienced entomologists can identify butterflies in flight based on colour, size, flying technique and so on. By and large, learning the jizz of animals sufficiently well to rely on

this knowledge in the field comes with practice, experience and dedication. The more time you spend watching wildlife, the better you will become.

Differentiating the jizz of animals can be particularly useful when conducting surveys or when trying to locate particular species for the purpose of taking photographs, and so on. Of course, it can also be useful in showing off your expertise and knowledge of wildlife to others, as an amateur, academic or professional naturalist or ecologist. Most of all, though, it provides a sense of one's own competence to know that such proficiency has been acquired.

Sketching, drawing and painting wildlife

As well as photographing or simply observing nature, it can be very enjoyable to employ artistic skills. Sketching, drawing, painting and even sculpting animals and plants can be done by anyone, regardless of the level of one's proficiency and skill. The important thing is to enjoy the process rather than worry about the finished result. This is because the process of creating art teaches you about the details of wildlife, both in terms of the design and the behaviour of species. The reason is that you cannot help but observe flora and fauna more intimately if you are trying to capture their essential qualities in a chosen artistic medium.

Birds are especially good for this, as they tend to have

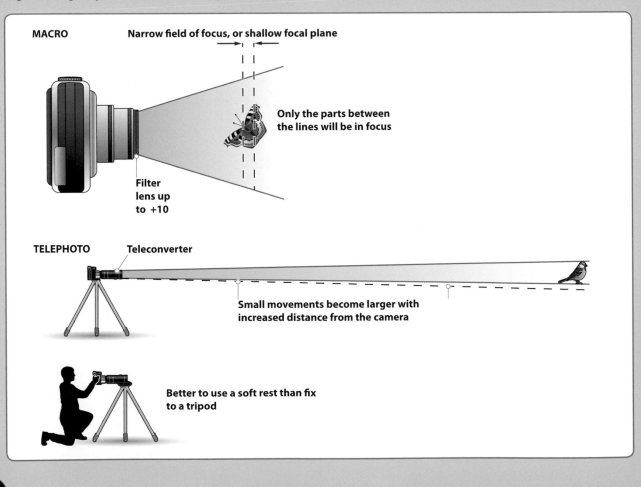

specific areas of colour and tone which are diagnostic of their species, and this makes for visually pleasing artwork. They can also be seen more easily throughout the year than other animals and flowers. In fact, a seasonal collection of artworks can be made to take advantage of the species most conspicuous in a garden over the year. The best advice is to give it a go and see how you get along. You may surprise yourself, both in terms of the end product and the execution. Drawing and painting is often relaxing because it focuses your mind on something other than the day-to-day concerns of life, just like playing a musical instrument or any other hobby. Your first attempt may not be as successful as you would like it to be, but that can be a good thing, as it will give you an ambition to improve with each new attempt. Progress is the name of the game!

Approaching animals to draw and photograph

In order to get closer to animals in order to watch, photograph, draw or sometimes catch them for study, it helps to understand the way they sense the world around them. In the case of birds, it is useful to use some form of camouflage or hide, so that they are unaware of your presence. If they cannot see you then birds are usually quite comfortable, as long as they see no movement and hear no sounds to give you away. Of course, in a garden the birds and mammals will often let down their guard if you simply watch them from indoors through a window. In fact this is a more convenient and comfortable strategy, which is why there are so many 'armchair ornithologists' in Britain. Just leave out some food and wait, with binoculars or camera to hand.

In the case of insects it is important to realise that you are not part of their world. As long as you approach with stealth, or simply sit still for a while, then insects will not notice your presence or be interested. Taking butterflies as an example, the main problem with photographing them is that they tend not to land for very long, and they are also inclined to move about while they feed. This presents a problem, as it is easy to approach them too quickly in an effort to get close enough before they fly on, with the result that you scare them away anyway. The solution can be to remain near the food plant and wait for the butterfly to return, or to keep pursuing the butterfly until it gets used to you and is no longer wary. You can often find that a butterfly will then 'pose' for the camera quite happily.

Another tip is to consider the time of day and the weather. Butterflies are often too active to photograph in bright sunshine, but they will take a rest when a cloud goes overhead. They also take a while to become active at first light, and slow down towards dusk. So think about behaviour and make a mental note of techniques that work and techniques that fail. Eventually you will become adept at stalking your quarry and come away with some impressive shots.

HOLE NEST BOX – BIRDS

This design of bird box is suitable for many bird species that naturally next in cavities. As birds vary in size, so it is possible to construct the same box by using different plank sizes – 5 inch, 6 inch, 7 inch, 8 inch, 9 inch and so on. The idea is to have a variety of sizes in your garden, to attract different types of bird – ranging from wrens to tits, to sparrows, to finches, to starlings, to jackdaws.

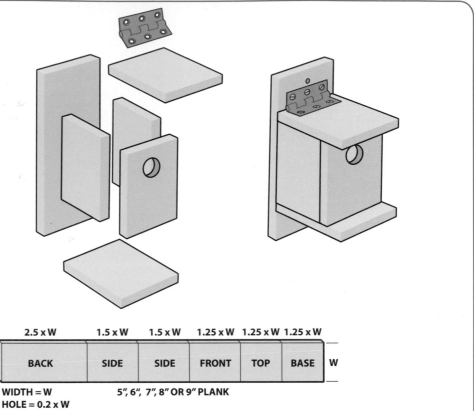

2.5 x W	1.5 x W	1.5 x W	1.25 x W	1.25 x W	1.25 x W	
BACK	SIDE	SIDE	FRONT	TOP	BASE	W

WIDTH = W   5", 6", 7", 8" OR 9" PLANK
HOLE = 0.2 x W
TOOLS: SET-SQUARE, PENCIL, TAPE, SAW, HOLE CUTTER, DRILL, SCREWS, NAILS, HAMMER, SCREWDRIVER

NOT TO SCALE

Kit:

In addition to the usual DIY tool kit, suggested on page 14, it will also be necessary to use a hole cutter to create the entrance hole. As a rule of thumb, the hole should be roughly a fifth of the width of the chosen plank size, so that it suits the size of bird appropriate for the box size. Always use a hole cutter with safety in mind.

Instructions:

1 Use screws or nails to secure the side panels to the back panel, making sure they are the same height, by using a set-square.
2 Fit the front panel, making sure it is flush and the top and bottom edges – cut the hole before fitting.
3 Fix the base panel in place.
4 Place the top or roof panel in place and draw a line on the back panel to mark the hinge point.
5 Use the hinge to mark the screw holes on roof and back panels.
6 Drill pilot holes and screw the hinge in place.
7 Use clout nails to fit a protective roof of polythene or DPC.
8 Drill fixing holes above and below the box.
9 Mount the box in a suitable spot, on a tree, a fence or a wall.

OPEN NEST BOX – BIRDS

Kit:

This box design requires only a basic took kit, as suggested on page 14, as it has no requirement for hole cutting. In addition, it has no hinge, so it is very easy to make the necessary components and to assemble them. It is worth noting though, that the open box needs to be placed in a safer location than a hole box, simply because weather and predators have easier access.

Instructions:

1. Nail or screw the side panels to the back panel, making sure they are the same height.

2. Fit the top and base panels.

3. Fit the front panel.

4. Use clout nails to add a roof covering of polythene or DPC.

5. Drill holes above and below the box.

6. Mount the box in place high enough and well hidden enough to keep the nest safe from weather and enemies.

This design of bird box is suitable for many bird species that naturally nest in recesses. As birds vary in size, so it is possible to construct the same box by using different plank sizes – 5 inch, 6 inch, 7 inch, 8 inch, 9 inch and so on. The idea is to have a variety of sizes in your garden, to attract different types of bird – ranging from robins to blackbirds, to thrushes, to doves.

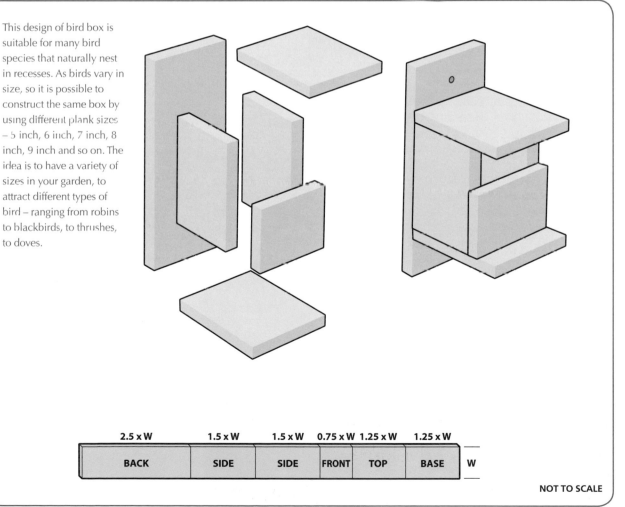

2.5 x W	1.5 x W	1.5 x W	0.75 x W	1.25 x W	1.25 x W	
BACK	**SIDE**	**SIDE**	**FRONT**	**TOP**	**BASE**	**W**

NOT TO SCALE

BIRD TABLE

This is a typical roofed bird table. It can be mounted on top of a pole or suspended on a chain, depending on your preference. Either way, it is suitable for a variety of garden birds.

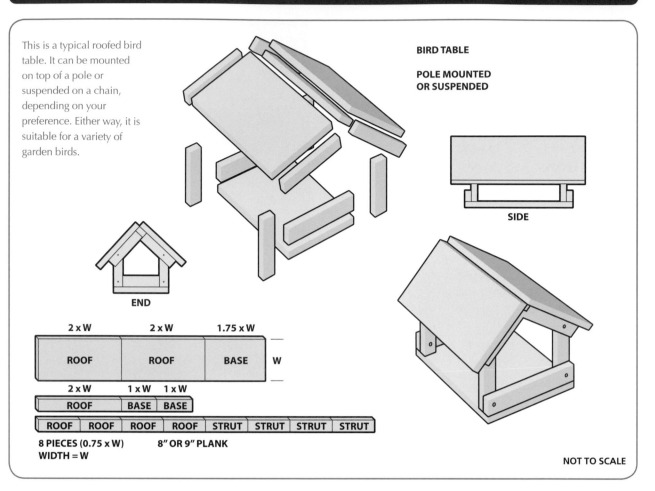

BIRD TABLE

POLE MOUNTED OR SUSPENDED

SIDE

END

2 x W	2 x W	1.75 x W	
ROOF	ROOF	BASE	W

2 x W	1 x W	1 x W
ROOF	BASE	BASE

ROOF	ROOF	ROOF	ROOF	STRUT	STRUT	STRUT	STRUT

8 PIECES (0.75 x W)   **8" OR 9" PLANK**
WIDTH = W

NOT TO SCALE

Kit:

Although this bird table has a number of components, the cutting and assembly is quite easy, so a standard tool kit should do the job – as suggested on page 14. We have suggested using 8- or 9-inch plank, with standard roofing batten. If you wish, you can improvise by using this design as a general guide.

Instructions:

1. Screw or nail the two base battens to the base panel.
2. Fix the four upright struts in the corners.
3. Fit the four-piece frames on each roof panel, so that they are flush with the leading edges at the top.
4. Join the two roof sections together, leaving a 'v' shaped valley at the apex.
5. Sit the assembled roof on the upright struts and secure the roof to the base section.
6. Use clout nails to fit a polythene or damp proof course covering, being sure to pull it tight across the valley at the apex of the roof.
7. Either position the bird table on a pole (by using a pilot hole and a large screw or nail) or hang it from a chain (by adding hooks at each end of the roof).

TREECREEPER BOX

Kit:

Although this box has a triangular cross section, there is no need to do any angled cutting – unless you really want to! A standard tool kit, along with a hole cutter, will be quite adequate for the task. You can use 5–7-inch plank, and the hole should be 1.25–1.5 inch diameter.

Instructions:

1 Screw or nail the side panels to the back panel, making sure they are the same height and they are fixed to the outside edges.

2 Slide the front panel in place and secure it, making sure the bottom is flush with the back panel and the top is flush with the top of the side panels.

3 Fit the lid – by either fixing with screws or with a hinge.

4 Use clout nails to provide a roof of polythene or DPC.

5 Drill fixing holes above and below the box, and then bolt in a suitably sheltered spot on a tree trunk.

Treecreepers naturally nest behind pieces of bark or in bow splits, so they favour nest boxes that mimic these tight conditions. This box provides a tapering or wedge shaped cavity to suit.

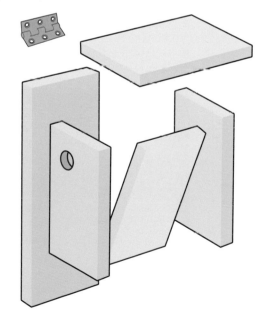

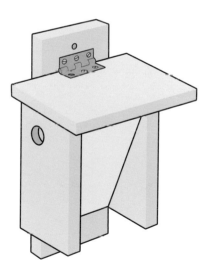

3.5 x W	2 x W	2 x W	1 x D	1.5 x W	
BACK	SIDE	SIDE / D	FRONT	TOP	W

WIDTH = W
DIAGONAL = D

NOT TO SCALE

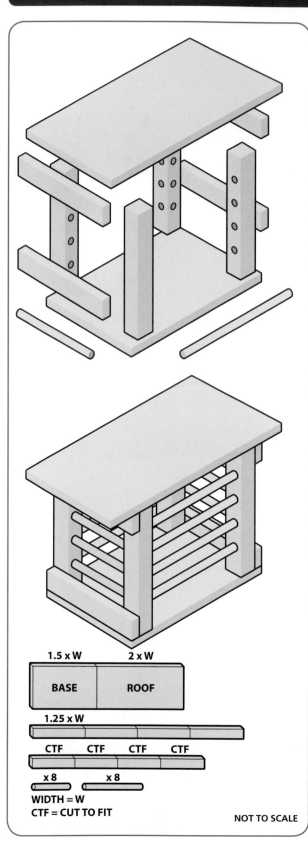

SELECTIVE BIRD TABLE

The purpose of this table is to prevent larger birds from hogging the food, as only smaller birds can fit between the bars. It also affords some protection when under attack by sparrow hawks.

Kit:

This build requires only a standard tool kit really, although some drilling is required for the bar holes. It is a bit fiddly to assemble, but not particularly difficult.

Instructions:

1 Screw or nail the pairs of cross-struts to the base panel and the roof panel, making sure there is an equal spacing top and bottom.

2 Drill holes with equal spacing along two adjacent sides of the for uprights, to suit the size of the dowel you have available.

3 Fit the first upright to the base panel and insert four of the long dowels.

4 Now locate the other ends of the dowels into the corresponding upright and fix it in position.

5 Repeat this procedure, going either clockwise or anticlockwise, until the 'cage' is complete.

6 Position the roof panel and fix in position – if you wish to attach the bird table to a pole then do so before you put the roof on.

7 Waterproof the roof by securing a layer of polythene or DPC with clout nails.

8 If you wish to hang the bird table, then attach hooks to each corner of the roof, and suspend from chains.

1.5 x W   **2 x W**

BASE   ROOF

1.25 x W

CTF   CTF   CTF   CTF

x 8   x 8

WIDTH = W
CTF = CUT TO FIT

NOT TO SCALE

WOODPECKER BOX

Kit:

In addition to the standard tool kit, a hole cutter is required for the entrance, so please follow the usual safety procedures, such a wearing goggles and making sure the wood to properly secured while machining. As woodpeckers vary in size, we suggest 7-inch plank for lesser-spotted, 9-inch plank for great-spotted and 11-inch for green woodpeckers. The hole diameter should be about a fifth of the plank width.

Instructions:

1 Screw or nail the side panels to the back panel, making sure they are the same height, by using a set-square.

2 Fit the front panel, making sure the top and bottom edges are flush with the sides.

3 Fix the bottom panel in place.

4 Affix a hinge to the lid and join it to the back panel so that it sits snuggly.

5 Use clout nails to add a waterproof roof covering of polythene or DPC.

6 Insert layers of cardboard, or stiff foam, until the box is filled to the top.

7 Drill holes in the back panel above and below the box.

8 Mount the box to tree trunk in a fairly high and sheltered position.

This bird box is essentially the same as the standard hole box, except that it is proportionately deeper to accommodate the cavity that woodpeckers favour. Inside, the box is filled with layers of corrugated cardboard or cavity insulation foam, so that the birds can excavate their own cavity via the entrance hole.

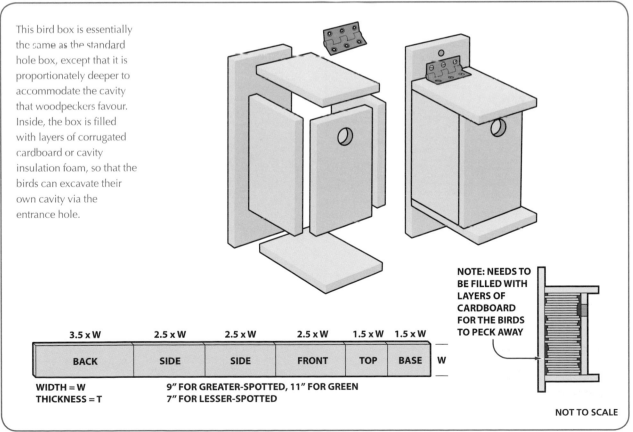

NOTE: NEEDS TO BE FILLED WITH LAYERS OF CARDBOARD FOR THE BIRDS TO PECK AWAY

3.5 x W	2.5 x W	2.5 x W	2.5 x W	1.5 x W	1.5 x W	
BACK	**SIDE**	**SIDE**	**FRONT**	**TOP**	**BASE**	W

WIDTH = W   9" FOR GREATER-SPOTTED, 11" FOR GREEN
THICKNESS = T   7" FOR LESSER-SPOTTED

NOT TO SCALE

HOUSE MARTIN BOX

Kit:

A standard tool kit will suffice for this project, but a hole cutter is necessary for the semi-circular entrance holes. As the diagram shows, the hole should be cut across the midline between the two front panels, prior to cutting them apart. We suggest using 6-inch plank and a 2-inch hole to give sufficient depth to the entrances.

Instructions:

1 Screw or nail the spacer panels to the back panel, making sure the spacing is exactly right for the front panels.

2 Slide in the front panels and fix them diagonally, so that the bottom edges meet the back panel and the top edges are flush. The spacers can be cut triangular if you wish, but it isn't necessary.

3 Drill fixing holes in each end of the back panel.

4 Mount the box in a suitable location, beneath the soffit board on a house, garage, barn or other outbuilding – as shown in the photo.

This project is designed to mimic the mud-cup nests that house martins naturally build below house eaves. Given the chance, they will often re-use old nests to save on effort and resources.

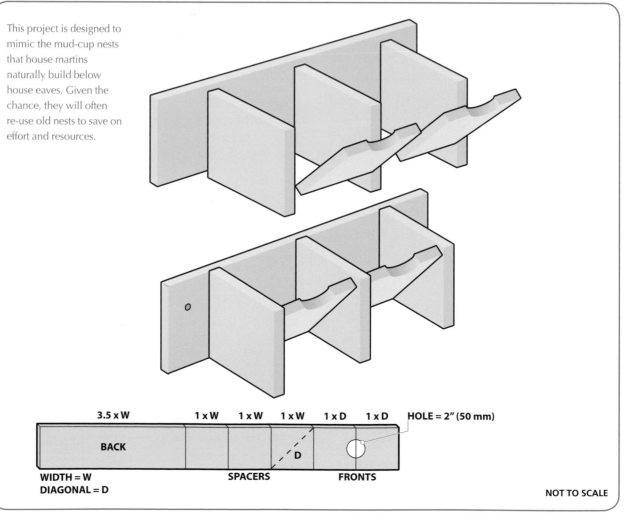

| 3.5 x W | 1 x W | 1 x W | 1 x W | 1 x D | 1 x D | HOLE = 2" (50 mm) |

BACK D **SPACERS** **FRONTS**

WIDTH = W
DIAGONAL = D

NOT TO SCALE

OWL BOX

This is really a proportionately deep open fronted nest box, as owls like to drop down into their nests. We suggest a 7–8-inch plank for little owls and a 9–10 inch plank for tawny owls.

NOTE: SLOT TO ENABLE BOLT TO BE POSITIONED PRIOR TO FIXING THE BOX

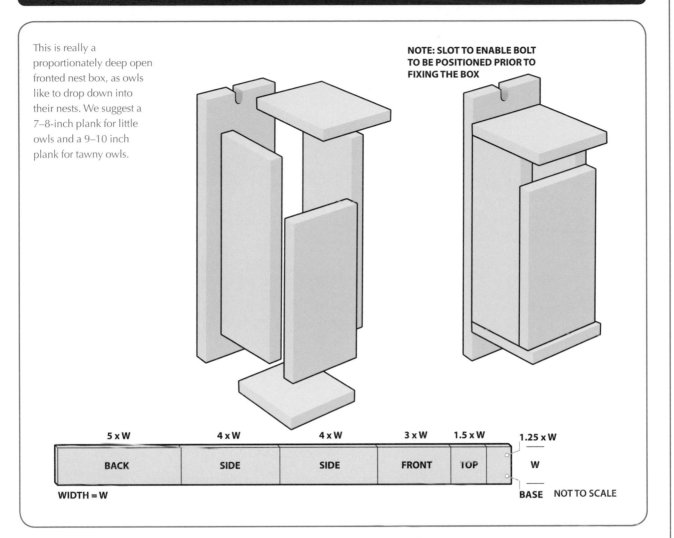

	5 x W		4 x W		4 x W		3 x W	1.5 x W		1.25 x W
	BACK		**SIDE**		**SIDE**		**FRONT**	**TOP**		**W**

WIDTH = W   **BASE**   NOT TO SCALE

Kit:

This project requires nothing more than a standard tool kit. The upper fixing hole is cut to form a slot for convenience and safety. It means that the back panel can be easily slid beneath the bolt head prior to screwing in the lower bolt.

Instructions:

1 Screw or nail the side panels to the back panel, making sure they are the same height.

2 Fit the front panel, making sure the lower edge is flush with the sides.

3 Fix the base and top panels in place.

4 Add a roof of polythene or DPC with clout nails.

5 Drill the fixing holes – cutting the upper hole into a slot.

6 Mount the box in a suitable location, on a trunk or bough with a slight overhang. Note: With larger bird boxes it is always necessary to put safety first when climbing ladders and drilling bolt holes, so always be careful and take your time.

SPARROW BOX

House sparrows like to live and nest communally, so a condominium nest box suits their requirements. Here we have three apartments, but you might decide to have four, five or six.

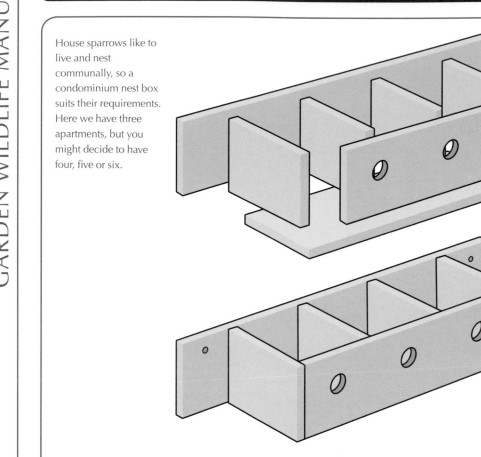

5 x W	3.5 x W	3.5 x W	1 x	1 x	1 + T	1 + T
BACK	**FRONT**	**BASE**			**END**	**END**

WIDTH = W
THICKNESS = T

SPACERS

NOT TO SCALE

Kit:

A standard tool kit will do the job for this project, with the addition of a hole cutter for creating the entrance apertures. We suggest using 6–7-inch plank, with a 1.5-inch hole.

Instructions:

1. Nail or screws the end panels to the back panel, making sure the space is equal to the length of the front panel.
2. Fit the front panel between the end panels and secure, making sure the front edges are flush.
3. Slide the spacer panels in place and fix in position, making sure the top edges are flush.
4. Sit the base panel in position between the end panels and the front and back panels, and secure.
5. Drill fixing holes in the back panel, each side of the box.
6. Mount in a suitable place below the soffit of a house, barn, garage or any other outbuilding – as shown in the photo.

WALL-MOUNTED BIRD TABLE

This design is for those who don't have a suitable place for a pole-mounted or hanging bird table but do have a wall.

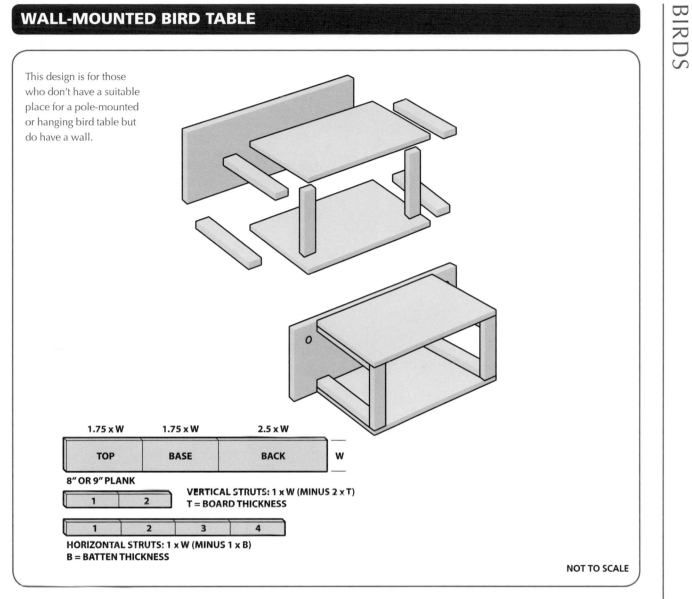

1.75 x W	1.75 x W	2.5 x W	
TOP	BASE	BACK	W

8" OR 9" PLANK

1	2

VERTICAL STRUTS: 1 x W (MINUS 2 x T)
T = BOARD THICKNESS

1	2	3	4

HORIZONTAL STRUTS: 1 x W (MINUS 1 x B)
B = BATTEN THICKNESS

NOT TO SCALE

Kit:

This project is about as basic as it can get, so a standard tool kit should do the job. Any plank size will do, but we suggest 8–12 inch, as there needs to be room for the food.

Instructions:

1 Fit the pair of side struts to the top and base panels, making sure they are flush with the rear edges.

2 Screw or nail the top and base panels to the back panel, making sure they are exactly aligned.

3 Fit the two vertical struts, and secure top and bottom.

4 Use clout nails to fit a waterproof covering of polythene or damp proof course.

5 Drill fixing holes each end of the back panel.

6 Mount in your chosen location on a wall – best in a location where the feeding birds can be watched.

Feeding birds

One of the most common pastimes for naturalists, amateur and professional alike, is to feed garden birds over the winter months. As well as supplying birds with nutrition, it provides a wonderful opportunity to watch birds that would otherwise remain hidden among the trees, shrubs and undergrowth of their habitat. It can be surprising to see what bird species will turn up at the promise of an easy meal, as finding sufficient food in the wild is often hard going. This is especially so during periods of prolonged sub-zero temperatures and snowfall, as more energy is required to keep warm and it is more difficult to locate sources of energy.

FEEDING BIRDS

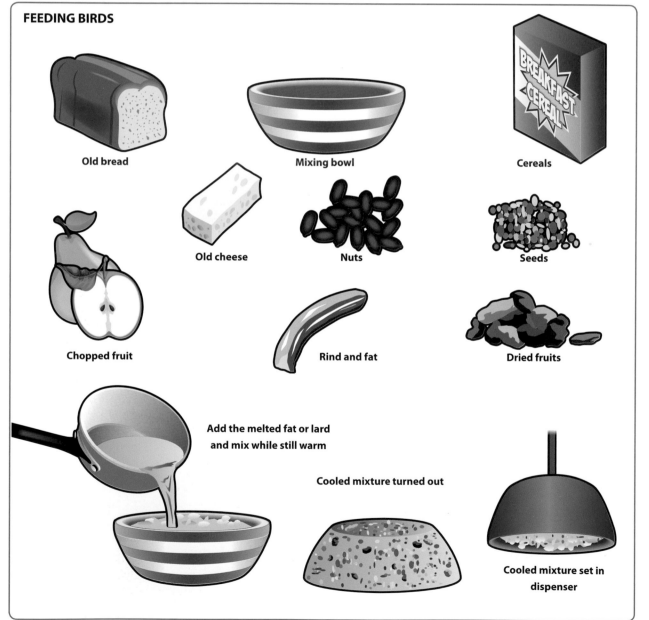

Old bread

Mixing bowl

Cereals

Old cheese

Nuts

Seeds

Chopped fruit

Rind and fat

Dried fruits

Add the melted fat or lard and mix while still warm

Cooled mixture turned out

Cooled mixture set in dispenser

It goes without saying, then, that birds favour foodstuffs offering compact calories, such as starches, sugars and fats. This includes nuts, seeds, dried fruits, bread, cereals, suet, lard, dripping, fatty rinds and cheese. That way a visiting bird can acquire energy in just a few minutes that would otherwise take a day's searching for in the wild. So it is easy to understand why birds find garden handouts irresistible, even though it may make them more vulnerable to predators, such as cats and sparrowhawks.

Rather than buying bird food it can be more satisfying and rewarding to make it yourself. The best way is to empty packet crumbs and stale provisions into a large bowl to create a general dry mixture. Melted dripping or lard is then stirred in to bind the mixture together. While it is still warm, the mix is then pressed into moulds where it solidifies into feed cakes. The set cakes may then be hung up within their moulds or removed and placed on feeding tables.

Bird brain teasers

Garden mammals and birds can demonstrate intelligence and resourcefulness in their efforts to find food. For example, before the age of modern packaging and homogenisation, blue tits were familiar raiders of milk bottles delivered to British doorsteps. They would peck holes in the foil caps and feed on the layer of cream.

It can be fun and interesting, therefore, to devise puzzles for garden animals, with the reward of food morsels. As wild animals are generally hungry at all times, they will invest a good deal of time and effort into solving problems in order to secure worthwhile prizes. The intelligence they reveal in so doing is what enables them to tackle similar challenges in the wild in order to stay alive.

Any behavioural advantage that improves a species' chances of survival and reproduction is favoured by natural selection, so the species is constantly updated by the process of evolution.

Wild animals can reveal themselves to be surprisingly clever at fathoming purpose-built challenges, and it is also fun to design and make the contraptions needed to test their mental and physical faculties.

Basic puzzles can be contrived by adapting readymade items such as plastic bottles and boxes, which makes life easier and reuses spent materials. The idea is that the mammal or bird can see the food item within, but has to work out how to reach it by performing a sequence of tasks rather than by simply breaking in.

Some devices unlock or open, thereby allowing the animals to take the food once they have figured out how to do it. Other devices reveal the food but close again when the animal attempts to grab it, thus requiring teamwork or exceptional cognitive ability. It is also possible to develop 'assault courses' to make it tricky for the animals to reach the feeding mechanism in the first place.

Kit:

A standard tool kit should do the job for these projects, but they do need to be made with some precision, so that they work properly. In the interests of using offcuts, please use these examples as guides for designing your own versions. The transparent plastic used is Perspex or Plexiglass, which can be easy sawn and drilled.

These three simple projects are designed to test the ingenuity of garden birds. The first one requires the birds to pull pegs to allow the nets to drop. The second requires them to swing a door to one side and the third requires them to use their own body weight to tip a door open.

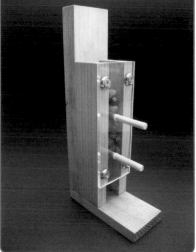

PULL-PEG BIRD BRAIN DEVICE

SWING-DOOR BIRD BRAIN DEVICE

TILT-DOOR BIRD BRAIN DEVICE

Pull-peg bird brain device

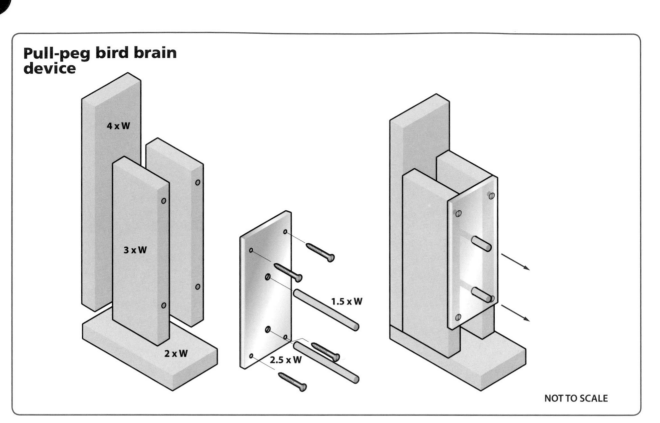

4 x W

3 x W

2 x W

1.5 x W

2.5 x W

NOT TO SCALE

Project 1. Pull-peg

1 Construct the body of the design by fitting the back and base panels and then adding the sides panels. You want a gap of about 1 inch, so that the pegs will prevent peanuts from passing either side.

2 The plastic front panel needs to be cut to fit the width and depth of the container, but leaving a gap of about 0.5 inch at the bottom, so that the birds can reach their prize.

3 The pegs can be made from 6mm dowel and need to be long enough to reach through the container with enough sticking out for the birds to grasp with their bills.

4 The peg holes should be a loose fit of 8mm diameter. They need to pass centrally through the front window and sit in holes drilled in the back panel.

5 The device can now be primed with peanuts and placed in position – either sitting on a horizontal surface or mounted to a vertical surface.

Project 2. Swing-door

1 This build is essentially the same as the first, except that a block of wood is required at the top of the cavity, from which the door can swing.

2 The door needs to be hung so that it can just swing freely from side to side, but prevent the birds from reaching their prize when it is closed.

3 Again, the device can be sat on a horizontal surface or mounted to a vertical surface.

Project 3. Tilt-door

1 This build is similar to the other two, except that it has a wider cavity, with a roof panel to prevent the birds from reaching down from above.

2 A sixth piece of wood is secured to the side of the body, to accommodate the door fulcrum and the door stop.

3 The door needs to be the same height as the box, but it needs to be about 2.25 times the width, so that it can tilt under the weight of a small bird.

4 Achieving the correct position for the fulcrum and the stop is a matter of trial and error. Drill the fulcrum hole a tiny bit over halfway along the door and about 0.33 inch from the bottom edge. Now fix with a screw and tilt the door to work out where to insert the stop. Adjust until it feels right – you can trim the door to adjust the weight balance if necessary.

5 The device can be fixed to a vertical surface or sat on the edge of horizontal surface, to allow the door to tilt.

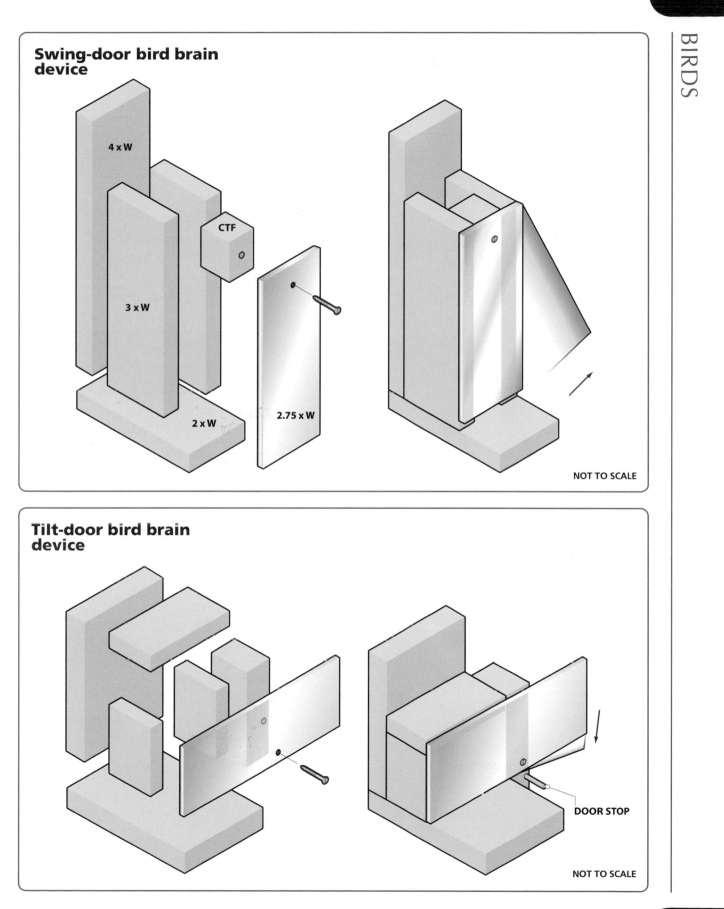

Swing-door bird brain device

4 x W

CTF

3 x W

2 x W

2.75 x W

NOT TO SCALE

Tilt-door bird brain device

DOOR STOP

NOT TO SCALE

INVERTEBRATES

The term 'invertebrate' is not a scientifically useful one, as it merely describes any animal that does not have vertebrae (a backbone), of which there are many groups. However, it is useful here, as it distinguishes from mammals, birds, reptiles and amphibians.

Most British invertebrates are known as arthropods. They are animals that have an outside skeleton (exoskeleton) rather than an internal skeleton (endoskeleton). The arthropods include insects, spiders, millipedes, centipedes and crustaceans. In addition to the arthropods, there are soft-bodied invertebrates that have no skeleton at all, such as slugs, snails and worms.

Collectively invertebrates form the foundation of the food chain, so it is important to have a wide diversity of species in our gardens in order to support a healthy ecosystem. This means having plenty of different plants and plenty of places for invertebrates to live.

▲▼ Orb spiders are the most conspicuous spiders in our gardens, because they sit in webs built in locations where flying insects are most likely to pass by. Females are far larger than males, as they are required to produce large numbers of eggs. The garden spiders (Araneus diadematus and A. quadratus) use contrast patterning to break up their outline, as a defence against birds. The wasp spider (Argiope bruennichi) uses mimicry instead, with stripes to imitate a large wasp or hornet.

Arachnids

By far the most familiar of the arachnids are the many species of spider and harvestman found in our gardens. The less familiar include mites, ticks and false-scorpions, which are generally smaller and have quite different lifestyles. Although all these different kinds of arachnid can be quite different in form and size, they share particular anatomical features. Unlike insects, arachnids have just one or two body segments instead of three, and they have four pairs of legs instead of three pairs. Other arthropods, such as woodlice, centipedes and millipedes, have many more body segments and pairs of legs.

Most spiders are predators of insects, but a few specialise in other prey, such as woodlice. Broadly speaking, spiders have three methods of catching insects in our gardens: wolf spiders and zebra spiders actively hunt by stalking and pouncing on their prey; orb spiders, and many others, use webs to ensnare prey; and crab spiders ambush their prey. Most spiders have a venomous bite to quickly immobilise their prey so that it cannot escape. The venom also breaks down the internal tissues of prey, enabling the spider to entirely drain the exoskeleton of its valuable nutrients through its fangs.

The most conspicuous spiders in our gardens are the orb spiders, as they construct elaborate, spiralling webs for catching flying insects. There are many species, but one of the largest is the garden spider (*Araneus diadematus*). The female is much bigger than the male, which is usual in spiders. This is mainly because she has to invest energy and nutrition into producing eggs, but it also means that the two genders tend to fill slightly different econiches in the same habitat to avoid competition, as the males build their smaller webs in places where smaller insects are more likely to fly. Both males and females wrap their prey in silk as a living larder, to be consumed when required.

Harvestmen will prey on small invertebrates when they can, but they will also feed on the juices of decaying carrion, fungi and droppings. Their long legs enable them to clamber efficiently through undergrowth, and when they find something to eat they simply lower their mouthparts down. This means they can avoid getting clogged up with sticky substances that might otherwise get them into difficulties. They are also able to shed their legs if they get stuck or if predators try to grab them, and they can get by with as few as two legs on each side. Unlike spiders, harvestmen are unable to spin silk.

Mites are typically very small arachnids, just one or two millimetres in length, although velvet mites and ticks can be considerably larger. They vary in diet, so that they include parasites, micro-predators, micro-herbivores and decomposers. Some mites are able to digest cellulose, which is the substance used in the cell walls of plants. They therefore play a vital role in breaking down organic matter as part of the nutrient cycle.

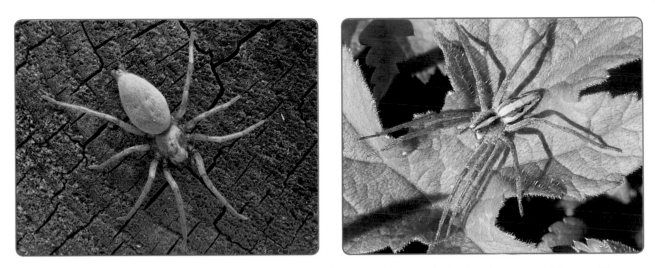

▲◥ Some spiders hunt for prey by roaming about our gardens. The pink stone spider (Drassodes lapidosus) is a nocturnal hunter, while the wolf spider (Pisaura mirabilis) is a diurnal hunter. Feeding by night and by day respectively means that the two species avoid direct competition.

▲▼ There are many small spider species generally known as wall spiders, as they tend to secrete themselves within crevices. At first glance they appear alike, but under magnification they have subtle differences. Those pictured here are the black wall spider (Coeletes atropos) and tabby wall spider (Segestria senoculata) varieties.

▲▼ Harvestmen are curiously simple arachnids, with just one body section instead of two. Their legs also have a very basic design with limited climbing ability. Their primitive form is nonetheless very successful. The varieties depicted are the rotund harvestman (Leiobunum rotundum) and the short-legged rural harvestman (Paroligolophus agrestis).

▶▲ The Teganaria genus of spiders includes the species commonly known as house spiders. In the wild they live in caves and tree hollows, which is why they are attracted by buildings, especially in the winter months.

Velvet mites are often the most conspicuous mites in a garden, as they are bright red and scurry about in their hundreds on walls and patios in hot weather.

Ticks are parasitic arachnids that feed on the blood of birds, reptiles and mammals, including humans. The newly hatched nymphs wait on grass stems and foliage for hosts to brush past. They then find their way beneath feathers, scales or fur, secure themselves to the skin with their mouthparts and siphon blood from the host until they are gorged and fall away with distended abdomens. Severe infestations can cause considerable blood loss in small mammals, and ticks can infect their hosts with viral and bacterial diseases, so it is important to carefully remove them when discovered.

False scorpions are so called because they have pincers like true scorpions. However, they are only a few millimetres in size and they have no stinging tail. They are essentially rather like predatory mites with pincers, that they use to hold their prey, which comprises even smaller invertebrates and their eggs.

▲ The gilded stretch spider (Tetragnatha extense) is a small web spider specialised in catching small flying insects, such as mosquitoes, gnats, midges and fruit flies.

▼ One of our more interesting spiders, the woodlouse-hunting spider (Dysdera crocata) has articulating fangs that enable it to seize a woodlouse in a pincer grip until the venom has taken effect.

▼ The zebra jumping spider (Salticus scenicus) is often seen hunting on walls, roofs and branches in the height of summer. It specialises in hunting by pouncing on small insects and demonstrates curiously mammal-like behaviour as it looks around and stalks its prey.

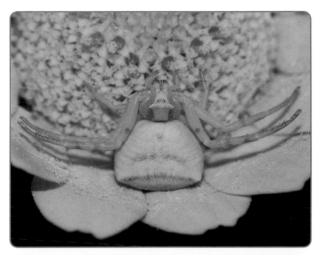

▲◥ Crab spiders are so called because their bodies are broad and their legs are set wide. This design enables them to sit undetected on flowers and grab visiting insects before they have a chance to escape. Pictured here are the goldenrod crab spider (*Misumena vatia*) and the triangulated crab spider (*Thomisus onustus*).

▶ Velvet mite (*Trombidium holosericeum*) adults are free-living, but their larvae are parasites of harvestmen. There are various other red-coloured mites to be seen in gardens, such as the red spider mite, which is a pest of cultivated plants, and the clover mite, which is often seen swarming over walls and paths.

▶ Ticks are parasitic arachnids, feeding on the blood of vertebrate animals. They are usually seen in their adult stage, when they attach themselves to hosts and gorge with blood prior to reproduction, looking rather like swollen balloons with legs.

▼ The pseudoscorpion (*Chthonius ischnocheles*) is a tiny arachnid that preys upon microscopic animals, which it seizes with its scorpion-like pincers. They are often overlooked, but can be quite common in leaf litter and humus.

Hymenoptera – bees, wasps and ants

The species from this order of insects include brown bees, bumblebees, cuckoo bees, true wasps, ants, ichneumons, parasitic wasps, spider-hunting wasps, sand wasps, wood wasps, sawflies, gall wasps and velvet ants. Despite the differences in size and appearance, these insects are classified together because they possess shared characteristics. They have either chewing or sucking mouthparts, and they have two pairs of wings, although worker ants and female velvet ants are the exception. Females have ovipositors – tubes for laying eggs – that are often modified into stings, used for defence or for disabling prey. Hymenoptera species also undergo complete metamorphosis as they develop, from egg, to larva, to pupa, to adult.

A number of species are notable for living socially, as this works as an effective survival strategy. In effect the individuals within the nest function as a collective organism, so that greater success is enjoyed with regard to the procurement of resources and defence against enemies. Solitary lifestyles bring other survival benefits, however, as populations are more scattered and therefore less susceptible to the depletion of resources and predation or disease en masse. So natural selection has favoured both strategies for contrasting reasons.

Intriguingly, ants, wasps and bees have developed different ways of making their nests, by utilising different building materials. Ants tunnel into soil to make the living chambers and passageways of their nests. If they need to add material then they stick grains of sand together with chewed mud to build walls. Wasps use decaying wood, which they collect from old tree stumps or fence posts and

▲ The yellow meadow ant (*Lasius flavus*) is responsible for building the mounds often seen in undisturbed meadows. The mounds result from the spoil excavated by the ants as they build their nests below ground.

then chew up to make papier mâché. This enables them to build lightweight paper nests for summer use.

Honeybees use beeswax to build their nests, which they produce from wax glands. It is a relatively heavy, tough and waterproof material, enabling honeybees to store food (honey) during the winter. This means that honeybees can survive the winter as a colony, while wasps die off to leave only hibernating queens. Bumblebees also use wax, but their colonies are far smaller, so they use the same overwintering strategy as wasps.

Worker ants, bees and wasps are all female, but they are not able to breed. Their role is to labour for the benefit of the breeding females or queens, so that their species benefits as a whole. The males of social and solitary species have no other role than to fertilise the breeding females.

▼ The black garden ant (*Lasius niger*) is the species that often enters houses in search of sugary foodstuffs. Once the food is located, the ants follow a scent trail to take the food back to the nest.

▼ The red garden ant (*Myrmica rubra*) is well known for its ability to deliver painful stings. This usually happens when people accidentally sit above the entrance to a nest, so that the workers attack.

A number of solitary bees make their nests in tunnels excavated from earth banks or rotten wood. They construct a series of chambers for their larvae, complete with sufficient food, and then seal the tube off. The fascinating thing is that the new generation of adults manages to emerge from the nest tunnel entrance in reverse sequence to avoid obstructing one another. This seems to be controlled by rising temperature in the springtime, so that the pupae undergo metamorphosis more rapidly the closer they are to the entrance.

It is possible to attract solitary bees to gardens by providing batteries of nesting tubes, made from bundles of straws, bamboo, or drilled wooden blocks. It is fascinating to watch them going about their business and they are very efficient pollinators of fruit trees and other plants. Leafcutter bees use sections of leaf to line their brood cells and can be seen flying back and forth from rose bushes and similar shrubs with large soft leaves.

Similarly, bumblebees can be attracted by installing nesting chambers. In the wild they use cavities in banks, in old tree stumps or beneath tree roots which are often abandoned rodent burrows. It is necessary, therefore, to bury artificial chambers so that the entrance is in a place where bumblebees would naturally search for suitable cavities.

Sawflies are often conspicuous in gardens because their larvae can denude plants of their foliage. They look rather similar to the caterpillars of butterflies and moths, but they have the habit of either raising their tails or curling them sideways when threatened. They also have nine or more pairs of legs, while caterpillars never have more than eight pairs in total. The adults look similar to wasps, but they are usually rather dull in colouration.

Two small species of parasitic wasp use the large white butterfly as their host. *Apanteles glomeratus* is responsible for the unsightly yellow cocoons that can be seen surrounding dead caterpillars still on their food plant. The larva of *Pteromalus puparum* pupates inside the chrysalis and then emerges by chewing an exit hole. Some parasitic wasps, from the *Lysiphlebus* genus, are so small that they parasitise aphids.

▲ The common wood ant (*Formica rufa*) is a large species of ant that typically frequents conifer forests, where it uses pine needles to build its nest mound. The ants spray formic acid as a defence, which smells like vinegar.

▲▼ A number of bumblebee species live in Britain. They can be tricky to identify because they show considerable variation in size and colour pattern. As they have large bodies and small wings, they have to put a lot of energy into remaining airborne, which is why they are often found stranded and exhausted on the ground.

▲ The honeybee (*Apis mellifera*) is unusual among bees, in that it survives the winter as a colony. In other species only the queens survive in hibernation. This is why they produce and store so much honey, as a food supply when no flowers are available.

▲ Although the leaf-cutter bee (*Megachile centunculus*) looks superficially like the honeybee, it is actually one of many brown solitary bees. The female uses pieces of leaf to line an excavated tunnel, within which it deposits eggs and food in a row of individual cells.

▶ Both the hornet (*Vespa crabro*) and the common wasp (*Vespula vulgaris*) are among the family of social paper wasps. They use chewed wood fibres to build their nests in sheltered places, such as holes in trees or below ground. Both species can sting, but they will only do so when provoked, as it is really a valuable tool for killing prey – which is why the sting has no barbs, unlike that of the honeybee, which is used solely for defence.

◀▼ Yellow-banded ichneumon (*Amblyteles armatorius*) and red-banded ichneumon (*Ichneumon suspiciosus*). Ichneumons are parasitic wasps that typically lay their eggs inside caterpillars, so that their larvae gradually consume their hosts from within while still alive.

◀▲ Bramble sawfly (*Arge cyanocrocea*) and emerald sawfly (*Rhogogaster viridis*). Sawflies are less well known than ants, bees and wasps, but they belong to the same insect order. Their larvae resemble butterfly caterpillars and can cause considerable damage to garden plants as they feed en masse.

◀ The larvae of the ruby-tailed wasp (*Chrysis ignita*) feed on the larvae of solitary bees of the Megachilidae family, such as mason bees and leafcutter bees. The bees tunnel into soft vertical surfaces, such as earthen banks and old masonry, where the wasp finds their nests and lays its own eggs. They are also known as cuckoo wasps, as they prey upon species of their own order.

▲▼ These two wasps are both known as wood wasps, although they are not in the same family. The long spine at the rear is not a sting, but an auger and ovipositor for laying eggs. The giant ichneumon (*Rhyssa persuasoria*) locates beetle grubs in rotten wood as a food source for its own larvae and drills down to lay its eggs using the entire device. The horntail (*Urocerus gigas*) rotates its ovipositor from a protective sheath, before drilling down to lay its eggs in the wood itself, as its larvae are wood-eating.

Coleoptera – beetles

Beetles and bugs are often confused with one another because they look very similar. In addition, many people incorrectly use the term 'bug' to mean any insect. However, there are distinct differences between beetles and bugs.

Beetles have a pair of biting mouthparts (mandibles) for chewing their food, while bugs have a single piercing mouthpart (proboscis) for piercing and sucking fluids. Beetles also undergo *complete metamorphosis* when they grow, which means that they go through a series of clear physical changes, from egg to larva to pupa to adult. Bugs grow by *incomplete metamorphosis*, which means that they hatch from the egg as nymphs, which are miniature versions of the adult form, and then go through a series of similar stages. Typical beetles also have their front pair of wings modified into hardened, dome-shaped wing cases (elytra), while those of bugs are leathery and flatter (hemelytra).

There are many types of beetle to be found in British gardens. They include ladybirds, leaf beetles, flower beetles, dung beetles, chafers, click beetles, ground beetles, rove beetles, burying beetles, weevils, bark beetles, wood-boring beetles, soldier beetles and pond beetles. In fact there are more species of beetle than any other type of insect, and they have evolved to exploit just about every econiche available, including water. They also range in size from the stag beetle, at around 75mm (3in), down to tiny pollen beetles at less than 2mm.

Within the many garden econiches, many different foodstuffs are exploited by beetles and their larvae. These includes dead and living plant matter – leaves, buds, flowers, wood, roots, fruits, fungi – and dead or living animals – carrion, caterpillars, snails, aphids, worms and so on. Some beetles are carnivorous, many are herbivorous, others are omnivorous, and the remainder have specialised diets, such as dung. There are also

▶▲ The larvae of both the stag beetle (*Lucanus cervus*) and the lesser stag beetle (*Dorcus parallelipipedus*) feed on rotting wood in tree stumps and standing trees. As their food has low nutritional value they take a number of years to develop. The adult male stag beetle is Britain's largest beetle, at almost 3in (75mm), yet it can fly. Beetles are able to fold their wings beneath their wing cases when not in use. This means that the relatively large wings needed to become airborne can be protected from damage.

nocturnal and diurnal beetles. The sheer diversity of species seen in beetles is the secret to their success as an insect order. They are therefore a good indicator of the ecological health of a garden habitat. If there are representative species from most of the beetle groups then it bodes well for the ecological community as a whole.

▼ The larva of the green tiger beetle (*Cicindela campestris*) catches prey by hiding in the ground with the top of its head at the surface of a vertical burrow. This unusual lifestyle means that the beetle frequents sandy soils, where it is easier to dig.

▶▼ There are many similar species of ground beetle. They come in different sizes, but they all have a similar streamlined shape, designed for ducking and diving beneath and between detritus. They are fast-moving and predatory beetles. They specialise in prey suited to their size, so that they avoid direct competition. The varieties depicted here are the violet ground beetle (*Carabus violaceus*), black ground beetle (*Pterostichus nigrita*) and granulated ground beetle (*Carabus granulatus*).

▼▶ The Devil's coach-horse (*Ocypus olens*) and the orange-black rove beetle (*Paederus littoralis*) are just two examples of the rove beetle family, which includes hundreds of species in Britain. Despite having very small wing cases, they have functional wings; they have short wing cases so that they can curl their abdomens forwards to spray a noxious vapour at enemies as a form of defence.

▲◀▼▶ Both the larva and the female of the glow-worm beetle (*Lampyris noctiluca*) have segmented bodies, rather like flattened woodlice. The male, however, has the form of a typical beetle and is able to fly to find a mate. Glow-worms feed on snails. They glow by a chemical reaction, which produces light but no heat. The two chemicals are known as luciferin and luciferase.

▼ The sexton beetle (*Necrophorus vespillo*) and the black burying beetle (*N. humator*), which is similar but has no orange, are specialists at finding dead small mammals and birds to bury as food for their larvae. They achieve this feat by gradually scraping the soil away beneath the corpse and by teamwork.

▼ The word 'dor' is an old English term once used to describe any insect that made a buzzing or droning noise. The dor beetle (*Geotrupes stercorarius*) flies noisily on summer evenings in search of mates and dung to feed its larvae. It is sometimes called the lousy beetle because it is often infested with parasites, which are actually mites rather than lice.

▶▼ The chafer family includes the goliath beetles, which is one of the world's largest beetles. The cockchafer (*Mololontha melolontha*) and the rose chafer (*Cetonia aurata*) are considerably smaller, but they are still large by British standards. They also have the front-heavy and barrel-shaped body typical of chafers.

▲ The bloody-nosed beetle (*Timarcha tenebricosa*) is a large leaf beetle found on the grassy margins of hedgerows. It gets its name from the fact that when harassed it exudes a reddish fluid from its mouth that looks rather like blood, smells unpleasant and tastes disagreeable to predators, which causes them to abandon their attempts to eat the beetle. The fluid is indeed the insect equivalent of blood, which is known as hemolymph. Other beetles, such as ladybirds, have a similar defence mechanism.

▼ Weevils are easily recognised by their elongated snouts, or rostrums, and their bulbous bodies. The pine weevil (*Hylobius abietis*) and the green nettle weevil (*Phyllobius pomaceus*) are typical members of the family, of which there are many species in Britain.

▼ Also called skipjacks, the click beetles have an interesting way of escaping predators. They fall to the ground and then activate a mechanism between thorax and abdomen that makes them fly into the air and land elsewhere, so that the predator looses sight of them. The red-brown click beetle (*Athous haemorrhoidalis*) is commonly found in gardens across most of Britain.

▲◀▼▶ The seven-spot ladybird (*Coccinella septumpunctata*) is the archetypal ladybird, though the harlequin ladybird (*Harmonia axyridis*) has recently invaded Britain from America and become commonplace. It is called the harlequin ladybird because it comes in a wide variety of colours and patterns, but it never has seven spots, so the two species can always be told apart.

◀◣ As can be seen by the colouring of the pale soldier beetle (*Cantharis pallida*) and the grey sailor beetle (*C. nigricans*), these beetles have their common names because they reminded people of the uniforms of soldiers and sailors in Napoleonic times.

▼ Many beetles are found on flowers because they eat pollen and nectar, but the cardinal beetle (*Pyrochroa serraticornis*) frequents flowers in search of smaller insects to prey upon.

▲▶ Both the wasp beetle (*Clytis arietis*) and the black and yellow longhorn (*Strangalia maculate*) are wasp mimics. Predatory birds believe they will be stung, so they leave the beetles alone.

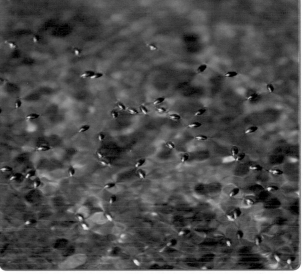

▲▶ Most water beetles, such as the great diving beetle (*Dytiscus marginalis*), live a submerged life in lakes and ponds. A few others spend their lives at the surface of the water, such as the whirligig beetle (*Gyrinus marinus*). The larvae of water beetles are also aquatic.

▼ The oil beetle (*Meloe violaceus*) is a flightless insect, whose larvae feed on bumblebee grubs.

▼ The violet ground beetle (*Carabus violaceus*) is so called because it has a delicate violet iridescence, making it appear quite exotic.

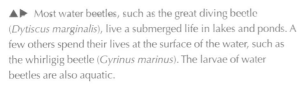

▲▶ The sloe bug (*Dolycoris baccarum*) and the green shield bug (*Palomena prasina*) are flat-bodied bugs, often seen on the leaves of shrubs. In America these bugs are known as stink bugs, as they emit an odorous substance to deter predators.

▼ The meadow plant bug (*Leptopterna dolabrata*) and the striped mirid bug (*Miris striatus*) are among many similar bug species with narrow bodies. They frequent grasslands, where they are well camouflaged.

Hemiptera – bugs

Although many people use the term 'bugs' to describe any insects or similar invertebrates, the true bugs have particular anatomical details that define them as bugs. They are insects with sucking mouthparts and leathery forewings, used to cover and protect their hind wings. They also develop as nymphs, rather than having larvae. However, true bugs come in a considerable range of shapes and sizes, often looking so different from one another that it isn't immediately apparent that they are closely related at all. They include aphids, leafhoppers, treehoppers, froghoppers, shieldbugs, flatbugs, fire bugs, squash bugs, stilt bugs, assassin bugs, damsel bugs, mirid bugs, pond skaters and water bugs.

As true bugs have sucking and piercing mouthparts, they feed on a variety of liquid foods. Many feed on the sap of plants, or the juice of fruits and fungi. Others are predatory, draining other invertebrates of their internal fluids. Water bugs may also prey on small vertebrates, such as fish fry and the tadpoles of frogs, toads and newts.

▲▶ Both the water boatman (*Notonecta glauca*) and the water diver (*Corixa punctata*) have modified legs that act as paddles for efficient propulsion through water. They also have large eyes, similar to those of dragonflies, which they use to spot prey.

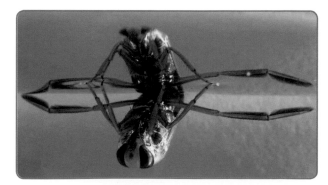

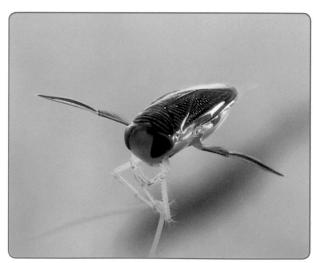

Shieldbugs are otherwise known as stink bugs, as they emit a pungent and rather unpleasant odour as a defence when harassed by predators or humans. Spittlebugs are actually the nymphs of froghoppers, which use shrouds of froth or foam, made from plant sap, as a form of defence from predators and from drying out.

Aphids are interesting insects as they have the ability to multiply by a process called *parthenogenesis*, which means without fertilisation of eggs. Nearly all of the aphids we see on our garden plants are female and they are able to reproduce without mating and viviparously, which means that they give birth to live young. In fact, the offspring are miniature genetic clones of females. The advantage of reproducing in this way is that populations can grow incredibly quickly, as they don't need to waste time finding mates and the young are born ready to begin growing, so that they too can reproduce in a matter of days.

As aphids are the prey of many other animals, including ladybirds, hoverflies, parasitic wasps, other bugs and birds, it is a useful survival strategy to be able to multiply in enormous numbers very rapidly. The drawback, however, is a lack of genetic variety for natural selection to work with, in adapting the insects to a changing environment. So in the autumn male aphids are produced, which then mate with

▼▲ The water scorpion (*Nepa cinerea*) and the water stick-insect (*Ranatra linearis*) are adapted to hunting much like preying mantises, with folding forelegs for seizing prey animals.

females to produce fertilised eggs. In the following spring, the eggs hatch so that the new stock of aphids has the genetic variation it requires to promote long-term survival.

There is also a fascinating relationship between aphids and ants. It is described as a *symbiotic relationship*, as both the aphids and the ants benefit. The ants provide protection for the aphids from predators, and in return the aphids feed the ants with a sugary liquid, called honeydew. Both the aphids and the ants establish this relationship quite naturally, so that it seems as if the ants are farming the aphids. Evidently this arrangement evolved far back in prehistory and has become part of the innate behaviour of both insects, because natural selection has favoured it due to increased chances of survival and reproduction, which is known as biological fitness.

▼▼ Most aquatic bugs hunt below the surface, but the water cricket (*Velia caprai*) and the pond-skater (*Gerris lacustris*) hunt by walking on the water. Their small size allows them to use the meniscus, or water-tension, as a hunting ground.

▲▶ Aphids, such as the black bean (*Aphis fabae*) and the apple (*Macrosiphum rosae*), have the ability to reproduce without mating, to save time, so that they can multiply rapidly and swarm while conditions are favourable. They then mate in late summer, to overwinter as eggs.

◀ ▲▼ Many bugs simply allow themselves to fall into the undergrowth when they are threatened. Others, such as the black and red froghopper (*Cercopis vulnerata*), the common spittle bug (*Philaenus spumaris*) and the horned treehopper (*Centrotus cornutus*), escape by hopping or jumping away.

Aphid microcosm

Aphids are able to multiply very rapidly, as they do not need to mate and they can give birth to live young. This means that, despite being very small, they offer a plentiful supply of food to other creatures. As a result many species prey upon aphids. Aphid predators include small birds, spiders, ladybirds, hoverflies and parasitic wasps.

Despite having so many enemies, aphids manage to remain so plentiful that their populations are not seriously affected by the onslaught. This is because, in addition to their rapid reproduction, they have allies too. These allies are ants, with which the aphids have evolved a mutually beneficial, or symbiotic, relationship.

When ants find aphids they proactively defend them against predators, because they have a vested interest in doing so. The aphids exude a sugary fluid, called honeydew, which the ants crave as a carbohydrate-rich food, so they do everything they can to ensure that the aphids remain safe. Thus both the aphids and the ants benefit from the arrangement.

As both instinctively behave in the appropriate way it is evident that their symbiotic relationship has been going on for so long that they are genetically programmed. In fact there is every reason to suppose that their symbiosis began more than a hundred million years ago when ants, aphids and many of their foes had already appeared on earth.

The way ants behave with aphids has been likened to humans farming dairy cattle. Although there are some apparent similarities, our relationship with cows is not symbiotic, as they don't provide us with their milk in exchange for protection from predators or any other benefit.

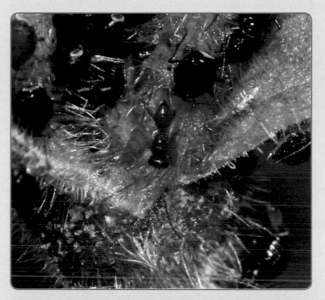

Lepidoptera – butterflies and moths

Easily the most popular insects in British gardens are the butterflies, which, along with moths, belong to the order Lepidoptera. Britain has relatively few butterfly species, largely because they are at the northernmost extent of their range, so most European species are unsuited to our climate. One only needs to travel to a meadow in France to realise how numerous butterfly species can be. Even in northern France, uncommon British species can be abundant, but that also says a good deal about the difference in the way the French manage their land, so that there are far more places for wildlife to live. In Britain butterflies survive; in France they thrive.

The popularity of butterflies undoubtedly has a good deal to do with the visual appeal of their wings. Like flowers, they bring splashes of bright colour in a natural world that is generally painted in dull greens, browns and greys. Also, butterflies are silent, they do not bother people, they cannot bite or sting and most are not pests, so they are well received in our gardens, unlike many other insects.

A number of butterflies overwinter as adults in Britain, so these are the first to be seen flying on sunny days in early springtime. The most conspicuous of these is the male brimstone butterfly, with its bright yellow wings. Consequently, the word 'butterfly' alludes to the brimstone, because it has the colour of butter. It was seen as a signal that winter was finally over – the season of the butterfly had begun. In mediaeval times the ushering in of springtime was very important, as it meant that people had survived the hardships of winter, where uncongenial weather and the scarcity of food meant a real risk to health and life. So the sight of a brimstone butterfly would have lifted the spirits considerably, and for many people today it still has the same effect, because it is still good to see the arrival of warmth and sunshine.

Butterflies and moths are unique among insects in having wings covered with scales. The original evolutionary function of the scales was to make the wings slippery in the mouths or predatory reptiles and birds, so that the insects stood a better chance of escape. Having evolved that way in the ancestral species, the wings presented themselves to natural selection with the potential to provide a wide variety of shapes, patterns and colours. As a result there are now thousands of species, each with its own wing design to assist in survival and reproduction in one way or another.

The majority of butterflies and moths are sculpted and decorated with hues and tones to provide camouflage as a means of hiding from predators. Others have eye-spots, or ocelli, to surprise and deter predators. Some have warning colouration, either because they are distasteful to predators or because they mimic species that are. Many also display showy primary and secondary colours that predators simply don't seem to associate with food, evidently because they imitate flowers.

There are a few anatomical and behavioural differences between butterflies and moths. As moths are largely nocturnal, their antennae are adapted to sense airborne pheromones to enable them to locate mates in the darkness. Some moths also use their antennae to find sources of food, although many moths do not feed at all. Their antennae are fern-like or feather-like to increase their surface area for these purposes, especially so in the males as they are usually tasked with finding the females as they sit and wait to conserve energy. Butterfly antennae, by comparison, are club-shaped, with rounded tips.

Another difference is seen in the typical resting posture. Moths usually rest with their wings flat against the surface on which they perch, whilst butterflies rest with their wings held together but will sometimes open them to bask in sunshine. This means that camouflaging is more often seen on the upper surface of moth wings and the undersurface of butterfly wings. As if to confuse matters, there are butterfly and moth species that are the exceptions to these rules. In France and Germany a moth is simply described as a 'night butterfly' – *papillon de nuit* and *nachtfalter* respectively – although that doesn't really work, as some moths are day-flying.

In Britain there are only around 20 types of butterfly that might be described as common or garden species, depending on where you live. The others are either localised in behaviour or they require very particular types of habitat unlikely to be found in gardens. Occasionally, though, a less common species may be seen because a colony happens to live nearby and individuals will wander in search of new habitat and new genetic stock with which to breed.

In the case of moths, the common species number in their hundreds, although far less is known about their distribution, for a number of reasons. As most are nocturnal and hidden by day, they are often overlooked. Also, as many are rather small and drab in colour they arouse little interest and can be difficult to distinguish from one another. Added to this, many species vary considerably in appearance so that identification can be fraught with difficulty, even supposing one has access to a comprehensive guide. As a result the larger and more colourful species tend to be the ones that get all the attention. It is a curious detail of the human condition that we give cachet to animals and plants that are more pleasing to the eye, even though less attractive species may be rarer and more interesting; but there it is, we are aesthetes by nature.

Butterflies are grouped into families, according to their relatedness. The generally white and yellow butterflies are Pierids. The generally brown butterflies are Satyrids. The diminutive gems (blues, coppers and hairstreaks) are Lycaenids. The moth-like skippers are Hesperids. The Nymphalid family contains the particolours, which includes the vanessids, such as the admiral and tortoiseshells, and the fritillaries.

Moths are similarly grouped into families. The Sphingids are the impressive hawk moths, with their sphinx-like caterpillars. The Arctiids include the colourful tiger moths and others with hairy caterpillars. The Noctuids include the yellow, red, blue and copper underwing moths. The Zygaenids are the day-flying burnet moths. The Geometrids include the famous peppered moth and others with looping caterpillars. The emperor moth, our only silk moth, belongs to the Saturnids. The Sesiids are the clearwing moths that mimic wasps and bees. The Cossids are the miller moths with wood-boring larvae. The Hepialids are the ghost moths with root-eating larvae. The Notodontids include the puss moth and the lobster moth, with their curious-looking caterpillars. The Tortricids include the codling and tortrix moths, with larvae that infest fruits, and the Tineids include the clothes and carpet moths, whose larvae feed on animal fibres.

The caterpillars of many butterfly and moth species can be reared in captivity for the purpose of education and general interest. In addition, adults can be released from captivity to augment wild populations. It is also possible to use ultraviolet lamps to attract night-flying moths, which are otherwise unlikely to be seen. Closely studying these insects it is a valuable insight into the biodiversity in British garden habitats and the biology of creatures that have evolved in very different ways to humans.

Butterflies and moths should not be 'collected' as they often were in the past, by killing and pinning specimens in cabinets. Not only is this unethical and at the very least politically incorrect, many species are in fact now protected by British and EU law. Advances in digital photography have made it far easier to take good photographs of butterflies and moths instead of 'collecting' them, so this is now considered the appropriate way to collect. The challenge of

▲ Probably our most widespread and common butterfly, the meadow brown (*Maniola jurtina*) often passes through gardens unnoticed because it fails to catch the eye. It has a lazy manner of flight and appears to be uniform brown. Upon closer inspection, however, the butterfly has a subtle beauty, with its muted tones and its eye spots. The caterpillar feeds on a number of grass species.

learning how to capture images of different butterflies and moths can be every bit as pleasing and rewarding as capturing them in the flesh, so there is really no adequate excuse for removing them from the ecosystem.

Butterflies: Browns – Satyrids

The browns are small to medium-sized butterflies, typically with colouring in different shades of brown and with eye spots, or ocelli. Their caterpillars feed on various types of grass. Most have a rather weak and relaxed style of flight.

▼ The hedge brown (*Pyronia tithonus*) is a livelier butterfly than the meadow brown and doesn't wander into open areas so readily. Instead it tends to frequent hedges and margins, where it is fond of sunning itself on bramble leaves and feeding from the flowers. It is smaller than the meadow brown and has noticeably brighter colours. The female is also larger than the male.

▼ The spangled markings of the speckled wood (*Parage aegeria*) mimic the dappled sunlight seen in woodland clearings, where this butterfly is often seen. It is quite conspicuous when it flies, but can be difficult to locate when it has landed. Each butterfly tends to have its own patch, and will investigate any other butterfly that comes by.

▲ The names of most brown butterflies allude to their typical habitat – meadow, hedge, wood, heath – and the wall brown (*Lasiommata megera*) is no exception. In nature it is found in places with exposed bedrock, but walls serve the same purpose. It likes to patrol stretches of wall in sunny places, where it can stop and bask in the heat.

◄ As well as heathland, the small heath (*Coenonympha pamphilus*) is found in areas of dry grassland and meadow. It flies in a similar directionless manner to the meadow brown, but cannot be confused because it is a much smaller insect and a much paler brown.

▲ Despite appearances, the marbled white (*Melanargia galathea*) is a member of the brown butterfly family. It frequents meadows, where it spends much of its time on the wing, occasionally stopping to feed from flowers. It is actually chequered rather than marbled.

▼ Gardens in heathland areas may occasionally be visited by the grayling (*Hipparchia semele*) wishing to feed on nectar. It is similar to the meadow brown, but its underwings are cryptically marked to camouflage the insect when it settles on patches of ground. It also leans towards to the sun so that it casts no shadow, making it very difficult to spot.

▲ The small tortoiseshell (*Aglais urticae*) is our most colourful butterfly, with its harlequin pattern of yellow, orange, red, blue, black and white. Yet when it closes its wings it becomes almost invisible, because its underwings are cryptically marked in blacks, greys and browns. Real tortoiseshell was once used widely as a decorative material because it displays various colours, which is how the butterfly got its name. There used to be a large tortoiseshell butterfly too, but that became extinct in Britain when the elm trees died out.

▼ The red admiral (*Vanessa atalanta*) gets its name from the orange-red and white bands set against black, which are reminiscent of the epaulettes on a naval admiral's uniform. The undersides of its wings have a wonderfully intricate pattern of colours, rather like an abstract painting.

▲ The beautiful eye markings of the peacock (*Inachis io*) are designed to surprise predatory birds that come to investigate when the butterflies are roosting or in hibernation. Like the small tortoiseshell, the peacock is one of the quintessential garden butterflies. It got its name from the exotic peacock bird, which was popular as an ornamental pet in high society gardens in Victorian times.

Butterflies: Particolours – Nymphalids

The particolours are large and robust butterflies, with a fast flight, mixing wing flaps with gliding. They generally exhibit bright and contrasting colours on their upper wing surfaces and have cryptic colouration on their underwings. The majority of species have caterpillars that feed on nettles. Their chrysalises hang head-down from plant stems.

▼ The white admiral (*Limenitis camilla*) can sometimes be seen in southern gardens near to woodland where honeysuckle grows, as that is the food plant of the caterpillar.

▲ The numbers of painted ladies (*Vanessa cardui*) vary greatly year on year, because these butterflies migrate from North Africa and the Mediterranean. The arriving insects produce a new brood in Britain in late summer, but they cannot survive our winters. The butterfly got its name from its showy colouring, as the term 'painted lady' was once a euphemism for prostitute.

▲ The comma (*Polygonia c-album*) is so called because it has a small white mark on its rear underwing that looks similar to a punctuation comma. In France it is known as Robert-the-devil (*Robert-le-diable*) due to its fiery orange-red colour and its jagged wing edges, which look rather like licking flames. In fact it is designed to mimic dead leaves, so that it can roost and hibernate unseen by predators.

◀ There are several species of fritillary butterfly in Britain, but the silver-washed (*Argynnis paphia*) is the one most likely to be seen in gardens, as the others are more localised and uncommon due to specific habitat requirements. The origins of the word *fritillary* are unclear. It may be taken from the French word *frétiller*, which means to flutter, as these butterflies are rather hyperactive. On the other hand it may be taken from the Latin word *fritillus*, which means dice-box, alluding to the chequerboard patterns of spots on the faces of Roman dice. As the other part of its name suggests, this particular species has a wash of silvery colour on its underwings.

◤▼ Both the dark green (*Argynnis aglaja*) and the high brown fritillary (*Fabriciana adippe*) are far less common than the silver-washed, but they are strong fliers and will sometimes visit gardens in search of nectar.

▲ Along with the large white, the small white (*Pieris rapae*) is commonly known as the cabbage white butterfly, because the caterpillars of both species feed on the leaves of brassicas. In this regard, they are the only British butterflies that might be thought of as pests, but only because we happen to enjoy eating cabbages too.

▲ When seen alongside one another, the large white (*Pieris brassicae*) is noticeably larger than the small white. Apart from this distinction, the two species are very similar in colour and marking. Their caterpillars are quite different, however, as that of the small white is a uniform pale green, whilst that of the large white is patterned with yellow, black and grey-green.

Butterflies: Whites – Pierids

The whites are medium to large butterflies with wings ranging from white to cream to yellow, and often embellished with darker markings. Their chrysalises are attached to the stems of plants in an upright posture, held by a silk girdle. Their caterpillars feed on a variety of woody and herbaceous plants, often crucifers.

▼ As its name suggests, the green-veined white (*Pieris napi*) has its wing venation accentuated with greenish-grey colouring. This varies between specimens but is usually sufficient to separate the species from the small white. The caterpillar is like that of the small white, but less often found on cabbages.

▲ Along with the brimstone, the orange-tip (*Anthocharis cardamines*) is one of the first butterflies to signal the arrival of springtime. The female has no orange and looks similar to the small white and green-veined white, but both sexes have a mottled pattern of mossy green on the underside of the rear wing, which is a very effective camouflage when the insects are at rest.

▲ The male brimstone (*Gonepteryx rhamni*) is an unmistakable luminous yellow colour. The female is pale yellow and easily mistaken for a large white when flying. As brimstones hibernate in winter, but are pale in colour, they have adapted to look like living leaves rather than dead leaves. Their wing venation is pronounced like that of a leaf and they always settle with wings closed.

▲◥ The clouded yellow (*Colias croceus*) is a migrant from southern climes. It is usually seen flying low and quite fast across open areas and it seldom stops to feed or rest. Its colour is a warmer yellow than that of the brimstone and it has a dark outer margin to its upper wings. Numbers vary considerably from one year to the next. As its name suggests, the less common pale clouded yellow (*Colias hyale*) is a lighter shade.

▶ The wood white (*Leptidea sinapis*) is a local species, sometimes seen in gardens adjacent to suitable woodland habitat.

▲ The male common blue (*Polyommatus icarus*) is like a living sapphire jewel when it alights on a grass stem and opens its wings to bask in the sunshine. The butterfly is highly active and difficult to follow when airborne, but the trick is to use one's peripheral vision until it decides to land. The female has a dusting of blue at the base of her wings, which varies between specimens.

▲ The holly blue (*Celastrina argiola*) is a noticeably paler blue in flight than the common blue, due to the colour of the underwings. While the common blue is an insect of grassland and meadow, the holly blue frequents hedgerows and woodland margins, where holly and ivy grow.

Butterflies: Gems – Lycaenids

The gems are small and dainty butterflies, often marked with iridescent colours on their upper wing surfaces and spots on their underwings. They have a rapid and unpredictable style of flying. Their caterpillars are grub-like and feed on a variety of woody and herbaceous plants.

▶ Although the small copper (*Lycaena plaeas*) is a very small butterfly it has considerable visual impact, because its iridescent burnt-orange markings stand out against the natural background of greens and browns. It is found in areas of scrub and ruderal growth where dock plants grow.

▼ A number of hairstreak species are found in Britain, but the purple (*Neozephyrus quercus*) is the most common and the most likely to be seen in gardens. Hairstreaks get their name from the fine streaked lines on their underwings. The purple hairstreak has iridescent purplish patches on its upper wings. It is seen flying around oak trees, which are the larval food plant.

▼ The green hairstreak (*Callophrys rubi*) is more widespread than the purple, but more localised. It lives in small colonies, sometimes on just one large bush, which may happen to be in or near a garden. Although some other British butterflies have green markings, this species is truly green on its underwings. The upper wings are chocolate brown.

▲ The large skipper (*Ochlodes sylvanus*) sits in an odd posture for a butterfly, with its rear wings held down and its forewings elevated, so that it forms an 'X' shape in cross section. This seems to be an adaptation to allow the insect to absorb as much solar radiation as possible, by exposing the surface of all four wings. It seems to be unable to spread its wings in the usual butterfly manner.

Butterflies: Skippers – Hesperids

The skippers are small moth-like butterflies of meadows, hedgerows and grassland. Their name alludes to their erratic skipping flight, which makes them extremely difficult to follow. Their caterpillars feed on various grasses.

▼◢ The small skipper (*Thymelicus sylvestris*) and the Essex skipper (*T. lineola*) are almost identical and often live in mixed colonies. The best way to tell them apart is to look at the tips of their antennae. Those of the small skipper are brown beneath the tips, while those of the Essex skipper are black. Despite its name, the Essex skipper is found over much of southern Britain, although it is not as widespread as the small skipper.

▲ The privet hawk moth (*Sphinx ligustri*) is Britain's largest resident moth species. The death's head, convolvulus and oleander hawk moths are larger, but they are occasional migrants from North Africa and the Mediterranean. When at rest, the privet hawk moth is surprisingly well camouflaged for its size, because its rear wings are hidden from view. As well as privet, the caterpillars feed on ash.

Moths: Hawk moths – Sphingids

Many of Britain's largest and most spectacular moths belong to the hawk moth family. They have distinct markings and long wings that call to mind the hawks and falcons of the bird world, hence their common name. Their caterpillars have the habit of raising the front portion of their bodies away from the food plant when at rest, which gave rise to their acquiring the scientific name Sphingidae, alluding to the Sphinx of ancient Egypt, which they resemble in posture. At that time there was great interest in Egyptology amongst the educated class in Britain, who were also the ones who studied entomology. In the US the moths are known as sphinx moths and the caterpillars are known as hornworms, because many have a thorn-like tail, which is quite harmless.

▲◢ The exotically coloured large elephant hawk moth (*Deilephila elpenor*) and small elephant hawk moth (*D. porcellus*) are so called because their caterpillars reminded the Victorians of the trunks of elephants. These species are common in British gardens because their larvae feed on willow herbs and bedstraws, which are ruderal plants that can readily be found growing in rural and urban places.

◣▼ Both the adult and the caterpillars of the eyed hawk moth (*Smerinthus ocellata*) and the poplar hawk moth (*Loathoe populi*) are very similar, and occasional hybrids occur. The rear wings of the eyed hawk moth have colourful eye-spots, designed to startle inquisitive birds. The poplar hawk moth has rust-coloured spots instead of 'eyes'.

▲ The lime hawk moth (*Mimas tiliae*) is beautifully marked with different greens and buffs, which have the effect of visually breaking up its outline to predators. Along with the eyed and poplar hawk moths, it does not feed as an adult, so it relies on its reserves of energy to find a mate and reproduce.

▶The hummingbird hawk moth (*Macroglossum stellatarum*) is so called because it does indeed resemble a hummingbird as it hovers in front of flowers, using its long proboscis to sip nectar. Most of the specimens

seen in Britain are migrants from the Continent, but the moth has been known to hibernate as far north as Bath, so that springtime breeding is possible.

▼The pine hawk moth (*Sphinx pinastri*) is similar to the privet hawk moth, but it is smaller and is not embellished with any bright colouring. It is the only British hawk moth adapted to feed on pine needles and can be very common in areas where conifer forest predominates. The caterpillar has stripes to mimic the food plant.

▲◀ Similar to the hummingbird hawk, the broad-bordered bee hawk (*Hemaris fuciformis*) and the narrow-bordered bee hawk (*Hemaris tityus*) can also be seen feeding on flowers by day, but they are far more localised. They are both bumblebee mimics.

▼▶ Hawk moths are great fliers, and occasionally southern European species such as the spurge (*Hyles euphorbiae*) and convolvulus (*Agrius convolvuli*) appear in Britain during the summer months.

◀▲ The garden tiger moth (*Arctia caja*) is brightly coloured as a warning to predators that it is distasteful. The caterpillar is armed with fine and brittle hairs that snap off in the skin of predators and cause an unpleasant irritation. Care should be taken when handing them, as the irritant makes fingers swell and itch.

Moths: Tiger moths – Arctiids

The tiger moths are representatives of the Arctiid family. The scientific name Arctiidae is derived from the Latin word *arctos*, meaning bear, because tiger moth caterpillars are hairy and often called woolly bears. The adult moths are called tigers, because they typically have black, white and orange markings – again, a Victorian point of reference to something exotic.

▼▲ The tiger moths bring a splash of colour to the British garden. Here we can the Jersey tiger (*Euplagia quadripunctaria*), the scarlet tiger (*Callimorpha dominula*), the cream-spot tiger (*Epicalla villica*) and the ruby tiger (*Phragmatobia fuliginosa*). The first three species are often mistaken for butterflies, because they fly by day and they have large colourful wings, which they flap relatively slowly.

▲ The peppered moth (*Biston betularia*) is a famous example of cryptic camouflage. It has been used to demonstrate genetic drift, which is part of the process of natural selection. In towns and cities the darker form is more common, because there are more dark surfaces to settle on, while in rural areas the pale form is more common, because the surfaces are not dirtied by pollution.

▶ While the adult puss moth (*Cerura vinula*) looks fairly ordinary, the caterpillar is quite unusual. It is camouflaged to mimic a folded leaf, but if a predator comes too close it puts on a threat display. It contorts its body so that a band of red is revealed behind the black head, complete with two eye spots, which creates the impression of the open mouth of a snake about to strike. The caterpillar also displays two bright red filaments from its rear end, which suggest stinging weapons to a predator.

▼◢ Although the cinnabar moth (*Tyria jacobaeae*) and the six-spot burnet moth (*Zygaaena filipendulae*) are not closely related they have evolved the same colouration, because red against black has become a ubiquitous warning signal to predators. Both species have toxins in their bodies, which predators do well to avoid getting in their mouths. In the case of the cinnabar moth the caterpillar also has warning colouration in black and yellow stripes. It is, however, eaten by cuckoos, so its stripes also act as a form of camouflage, by mimicking the pattern created by the yellow petals of its food plant, ragwort, set against a dark background.

▶ The adult lobster moth (*Stauropus fagi*) is cryptically coloured to match the bark of trees and even has fringed wing edges to blur the boundary between moth and tree. The caterpillar is remarkable as a mimic. When small it looks very much like a red ant, which predatory birds leave alone to avoid being stung. When it grows larger it is able to fold its abdomen over to mimic a large spider, which predatory birds will also leave alone to avoid being bitten.

Moth camouflage, warning and mimicry

All moths defend themselves from predators in one way or another. Evolution has adapted their appearance and behaviour, because those that have survived have passed on their genes to each new generation. This is a process known as natural selection, because nature tends to select the specimens that are best suited to their environment, which includes the avoidance of being eaten.

The most common form of defence is called cryptic camouflage, where the moth blends into its surroundings. The colouring and shape of the moth make it difficult for predators to see it against the background. Behaviour is important too, as the moth needs to land in the right place and then position itself correctly.

Some moths don't use camouflage at all. Instead, they have bright and contrasting colours that warn predators that they taste unpleasant. A few individuals die because predators need to learn from their mistakes, but most survive. This is called aposematic colouration.

Other species of moth have adapted to imitate or mimic the poisonous species, because predators cannot tell them apart. There are also moths that are brightly coloured to mimic flowers, so that birds can see them quite easily but overlook them. In the case of caterpillars the same rules apply, so that there are many variations on the themes of camouflage, warning and mimicry in both the adult and larval stages of moths.

▼ All of the underwing moths are cryptically coloured, to hide away unseen in leaf litter. If they are disturbed by predators they are quick to escape, and as they fly they expose flashes of colour on their rear wings that momentarily distract the eye, so that predators are disconcerted. The term 'underwing' is a misnomer, as it is its hind upper wing that has the bright colour.

◄ The red underwing (*Catocala nupta*) is one of our largest and most beautiful moths, with a wingspan of around 3in (80mm). The caterpillar is a master of camouflage, hiding itself during the day on the bark of the tree on which it feeds.

▼ **1** Drinker (*Euthrix potatoria*), **2** swallow prominent (*Pheosia tremula*), **3** oak eggar (*Lasiocampa quercus*), **4** coxcomb prominent (*Ptilodon capucina*), **5** pale prominent (*Pterostoma palpina*), **6** mullein (*Cucullia verbasci*) and **7** bufftip (*Phalera bucephala*). All of these moths mimic detritus found in woodland, such as dead leaves, fallen twigs and peeling bark. There is a certain amount of luck involved with simply blending into the background, so actually resembling a piece of debris can be a better way to fool predatory eyes. That way, it doesn't matter exactly where the moth decides to land, as long as it is in roughly the right place.

Marvellous miscellaneous moths

Some moths are celebrated by naturalists for their beauty. It is fair to say that most moths are rather dull and uninteresting to look at, so the human eye is instinctively drawn towards those that appeal to our visual sensibilities. It doesn't mean they are any more important, but it is human nature to prize animals that possess colours and patterns that excite the retina a bit more than the ordinary. A child's interest in nature is often initiated by the discovery of an insect that looks exotic, weird or wonderful, not least because its beauty is realised by the kind of close scrutiny that children are wont to give.

The wings of moths and butterflies are miniature works of art that have a natural beauty because evolution uses the patterns of colour for various different reasons to benefit the survival and reproduction of each species. They are beautiful to us, but to the insects they are a matter of biological fitness in a world where their design is all about keeping the species extant and passing on genes to the next generation. Each species is different because natural selection has found a different solution to the same problem.

▼ Moths come in a vast array of different colours, patterns and shapes. They are rather like miniature works of art. See if you can identify these six common species.

Christmas moths

In the depths of winter most insects are in hibernation, either as eggs, larvae, pupae or adults. However, just a few species are active at this time, including a few species of moth, such as the winter moth (*Operophtera brumata*), the mottled umber (*Erannis defoliaria*) and the December moth (*Poecilocampa populi*). These moths have chemicals in their blood to prevent them from freezing when temperatures fall below 0°C. The mottled umber and winter moths are small-bodied moths that use very little energy to fly, but the December moth is a large-bodied moth and is reluctant to fly as it wastes the energy it needs to reproduce. In order to fly it needs to warm its flight muscles by shivering until it is able to flap its wings fast enough to take off.

▲ Mottled umber moth.

▼ Winter and December moths side-by-side!

▼ December moth.

Butterfly bush

It is fair to say that buddleia has become a ubiquitous and invasive weed across much of Britain, so many naturalists dislike the plant for spoiling the ecological balance in natural habitats. While it is true that buddleia should be removed from genuine areas of natural habitat for the sake of preserving native species, there is some argument that it is a useful addition to the artificial habitats found in our gardens and parks. This is because buddleia provides copious amounts of nectar for insects in a relatively small space.

In fact buddleia is so attractive to nectar-feeding insects that it can be interesting to keep a record of the number of species seen on a single shrub over a season. Also, due to the presence of these insects a number of predators are attracted too. During the day, dragonflies may prowl the airspace in search of an easy meal. During the night, bats may patrol in search of nocturnal insects. As well as the number of insect

species, it can be remarkable how many insects are feeding on a buddleia at a given moment. Sometimes scores of butterflies and bumblebees will swarm over a buddleia bush.

Breeding butterflies and moths

Perhaps the best way to study nature is to keep small animals in captivity. Many types of animal can be reared and bred, but here we focus on moths and butterflies, as they are generally easy and convenient to look after. As well as learning about how they grow and live, raising species in captivity has its benefits as it gives them a better chance of survival than they would have in the wild. This is because predators, parasites and disease are removed, and poor weather conditions are eliminated. Thus stock can be released back into the environment to supplement garden populations.

The best moth and butterfly species to choose are the larger ones, as they are more robust and therefore easier to handle without harming them. In addition, they are more impressive and interesting to look at. In any case, the caterpillars found most easily tend to be those conspicuous by their size.

Many containers can be used to house caterpillars – glass jars, plastic tubs, cardboard boxes, mesh cages and so on. The main things to consider are that the caterpillars remain ventilated and dry, and that they are kept warm, but not too hot. It is also important to clean out their accommodation regularly and frequently, to avoid a build-up of waste.

The correct food plant must be provided, either as cut stems or as a potted plant. It is best not to put the stems in water, however, as that can result in the caterpillars consuming too much fluid, which leads to death.

Although there are exceptions, generally speaking butterfly caterpillars pupate by attaching themselves to dry plant stems above ground, while moth caterpillars pupate by burying themselves in surface soil and leaf litter. So it is necessary to provide them with what they need to turn into chrysalises. Similarly, they require something to crawl up when they emerge from their chrysalises as adults, so that the insects can expand and dry their wings.

Once ready to fly, adult moths and butterflies require larger cages. Moths tend to be easier to pair and mate, as they do not have courtship flights and are instead strongly attracted to one another by sexual scents called pheromones. Some butterflies will mate if given sufficient space, sunlight, nectar and food plants, but many will not.

Of course, each species of moth and butterfly is different from the last in terms of its exact idiosyncrasies, but most can be successfully reared and bred in captivity with little experience, as long as the basic rules are observed. It is really common sense for the most part, as the idea is to imitate the congenial conditions favoured by the insects in their natural habitat.

Note that it is illegal to disturb, buy or own species of butterfly or moth that are protected by law, so always check the legal situation before embarking on a breeding project.

MOTH AND BUTTERFLY BREEDING CAGE

When I was a boy I made breeding cages in all shapes and sizes, depending on the offcuts and scraps of timber I had available. This project is designed to use just planks, batten and slats of wood. The width of plank used will determine the overall size of the cage, so the wider the better. Of course, you can design your own cage if you prefer, but this one is relatively quick and easy to build.

Kit:

Although this projects has many components, they are all straightforward to measure, cut and assemble, so a standard tool kit should be all you need for the job in hand. The cage netting is a fabric named tulle, but any fine netting will do – black is best, as it is easier to see through.

Instructions:

1 Screw or nail the side panels to the ends of the floor panel.

2 Fix the upper back panel between the side panels, flush with the top edges.

3 Fit the door (lower back) panel, with a hinge and bolt – it also needs a stop strut at the end opposite the hinge.

4 Fix the battens to the top and front edges of the sides panels, making sure there is room for the three cross struts.

5 Fix the upper front cross-strut in place.

6 The other two struts need to be removable, as they hold the ends of the netting, so fit them with screws into each end through the side panels.

7 Install the netting by rolling one end around the front lower strut and screwing in position. Then pull the netting over and wrap the other end round the upper rear strut.

8 Finally, fit wooden slats over the front and top corners, to clamp the side edges of the netting in place.

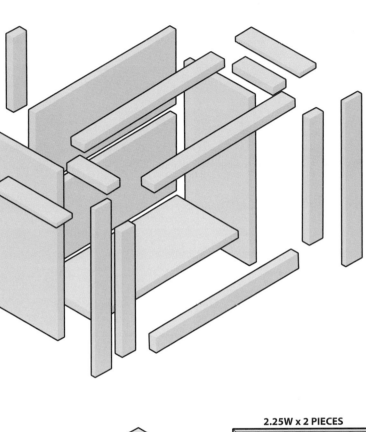

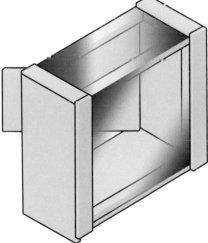

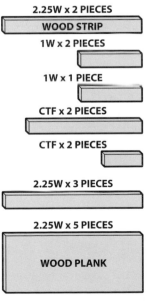

2.25W x 2 PIECES
WOOD STRIP

1W x 2 PIECES

1W x 1 PIECE

CTF x 2 PIECES

CTF x 2 PIECES

2.25W x 3 PIECES

2.25W x 5 PIECES
WOOD PLANK

NOT TO SCALE

These netting sleeves are used for rearing caterpillars on potted plants or the branches of trees. They are about the same size as a pillow case, with a draw string at the open end, so that they can be secured tightly. This prevents predators getting in, as well as the caterpillars from getting out.

BUTTERFLY HIBERNATION BOX

It is quite common to find small tortoiseshells, peacocks and red admirals hibernating in sheds and outbuildings. This box is designed to give them somewhere else to hibernate, and somewhere to put them if they are discovered by accident during a winter clear out.

Kit:

This box is about as basic as it gets – just square cuts – so a standard tool kit will do the job nicely.

Instructions:

1 Screw or nail the side panels to the back panel, making sure they are level with a set-square.
2 Fit the top and bottom panels in place.
3 Fix the front panel, leaving a gap at the bottom, for the butterflies to walk inside.
4 Use clout nails to secure a roof of polythene or DPC.
5 Drill fixing holes above and below the box.
6 Attach the box to the wall of a shed or outhouse, in a sheltered but visible spot.

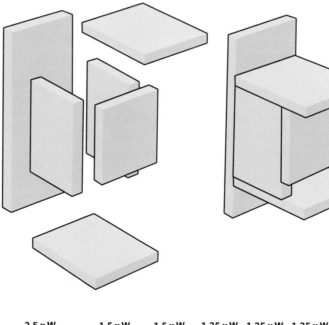

2.5 x W	1.5 x W	1.5 x W	1.25 x W	1.25 x W	1.25 x W	
BACK	SIDE	SIDE	FRONT	FRONT	FRONT	W

WIDTH = W   6", 7", 8" OR 9" PLANK

NOT TO SCALE

Mothing

It is possible to attract moths by a number of means, but the best way is by using a light trap. Many moths will be attracted by normal light bulbs, which is why they are often found settled by security lights, porch lights and window lights. However, the best type of light to use is ultraviolet, because this is the part of the light spectrum that insects see best.

There is a good deal of contention as to exactly why moths are attracted to light. The received wisdom has it that moths navigate by using the moon as a fixed point of reference, so that they confuse an artificial light with the moon and fly round in circles in an effort to keep the 'moon' at the same bearing, until they find themselves too confused to keep flying. As moths still travel when the sky is overcast this explanation seems flawed, especially as they are usually male moths following female scent trails, which randomly drift in the air.

So it seems that moths are not attracted by lights as such but become entranced by them when they happen to fly past en route to somewhere else. The most scientifically sound explanation is that night-flying moths respond to light by seeking somewhere dark to conceal themselves, because they think the daytime has arrived. Rather than fly away from the light as one might expect, the contrast between the light and the background means that they instead head for the boundary between brightness and darkness, which results in them perpetually flying round in circles, trying to keep the light orientated above and the dark below.

As daylight contains high levels of ultraviolet light, then it makes sense that ultraviolet lamps entrance moths more effectively than other sources of artificial light. To them the day has arrived, and they need to conceal themselves from predators until the next nightfall. Once they have alighted they instinctively settle and remain still, even though they have failed to escape the light. In fact, many moths will fly away when the real day arrives because the all-encompassing light frees them from their disorientation, so that they can seek out genuine places to hide.

This is why it is useful to have a light trap with a chamber in which the moths can settle. During the night, when the ultraviolet light is most effective, the moths are beguiled into thinking they are sheltering safely, because they can still see the light source at a distance. When the real daylight comes, they think exactly the same thing, so they stay put instead of having any desire to relocate themselves.

As we have established, it is not necessary to go mothing on a clear night with the moon in view. What is important is that the weather has been dry and warm and continues to

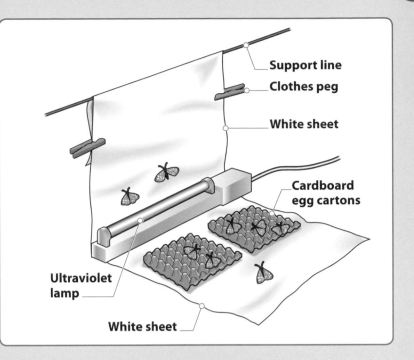

Support line
Clothes peg
White sheet
Cardboard egg cartons
Ultraviolet lamp
White sheet

be so. That way more moths are likely to have emerged from their pupae and more moths are likely to be active. As the moths will be attracted to a light trap in passing, it is necessary to optimise moth traffic by choosing the right conditions. The majority will be male moths preoccupied with following the pheromone trails of females, although females may also be on the wing having already mated and set off to find suitable food plants for laying eggs.

It is well worth attending moth traps during the night, so that new arrivals can be enjoyed as they circle and land. Above all it is an educational way to spend a few hours. However, with a decent trap it is possible to retire for the night and examine the catch in the morning. Generally speaking, small moths can be tricky to observe in daylight because they readily take flight when disturbed. Larger moths are reluctant to fly because they have a vested interest in conserving their energy. They need time and effort to warm up their wing muscles, and lifting a heavy body into the air takes a good deal of fuel, so they would much rather stay put unless they feel threatened enough to leave.

Some moths can also be attracted by spreading sugary concoctions onto the bark of trees, which act as lures. The moths detect the scent and come to feed, just as they naturally do on the juices of fallen fruits, carrion and nectar. There are many tried and tested recipes for this, but it is worth experimenting with the ingredients. Broadly speaking it needs to be sweet to the taste and have an aroma that will carry on the breeze. A touch of alcohol can help, as ethanol is found in fermenting fruits, so the moths have evolved to find it attractive. Of course, it is also possible to plant flowers with heady perfumes and abundant nectar, although many moth species are not interested in feeding at all. They just get on with the business of reproduction by using the energy reserves inherited from their larval stage.

MOTH UV-LIGHT TRAP BOX

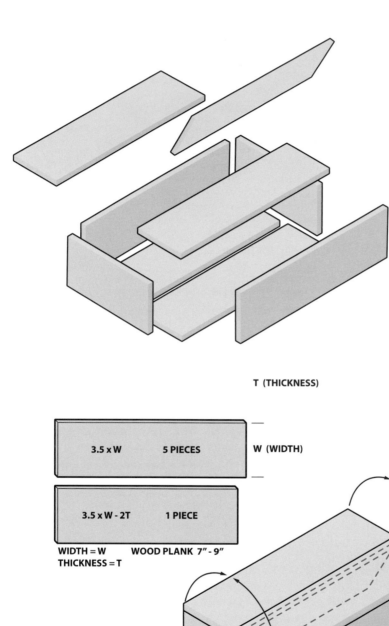

This project may seem complicated, but it is actually quite simple, involving only square cuts. It is a self-contained and portable unit. Moths are attracted to the screen and they fall down into a holding chamber, where they then settle.

Kit:

The actual build requires nothing more than a standard tool kit. In addition, you will need various pieces of door furniture, such as hinges, bolts, clasps and a handle. The lamp is a standard unit for aquariums and vivariums, which comes in various lengths, so determining the exact dimensions of the box required. The screen is a silver-fabric sprung roller blind, with an adjustable tent prop for support. The egg boxes are the paper type. This particular example uses a 550mm UV unit and 7-inch planking.

T (THICKNESS)

3.5 x W	5 PIECES

W (WIDTH)

3.5 x W - 2T	1 PIECE

WIDTH = W WOOD PLANK 7" - 9"
THICKNESS = T

2 x W -T	2 PIECES

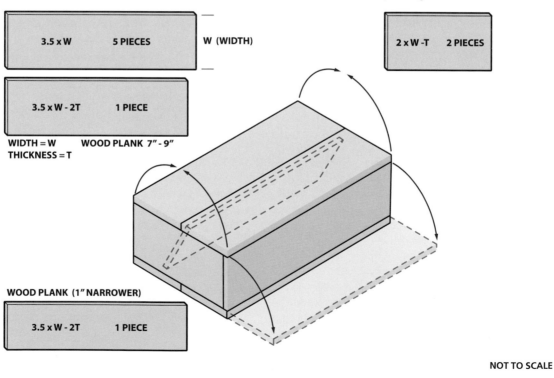

WOOD PLANK (1" NARROWER)

3.5 x W - 2T	1 PIECE

NOT TO SCALE

1. Screw or nail the two base panels to the side panel to form the basic shape, leaving a lip at the front edge of the base.
2. Fit the back panel, on top of the base panel and between the end panels to form a box.
3. Fix the front top panel in place, so that it has the same lip at the front as the base, to accommodate the chamber door.

4. Adjoin the rear top panel with hinges, so that it opens forwards to lie flat on the box.
5. Fit the chamber door at the front, so that it has a snug fit but easily swings open when required – this may require a little trimming.
6. Fit the UV unit to the inside surface of the top door.
7. Fix the roller blind (which may require trimming to width) to the base at the rear of the box.

8. Drill a hole in the leading edge of the back panel to accommodate the tent prop.
9. Insert and fix the partitioning panel, at an angle, so that moths will fall through the space between the panel and the screen, into the holding chamber.
10. Fit the necessary bolts, clasps and handle – plus some rubber feet on the undersurface.

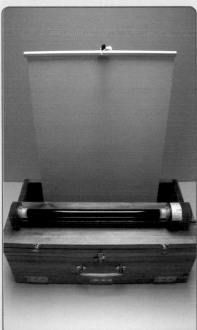

Odonata – dragonflies and damselflies

The insect order Odonata includes some of our most spectacular insects, both in size and colouration, for these are the dragonflies and damselflies. The fundamental difference between dragonflies and damselflies is that the former are rather stockier in build than the latter. Dragonflies are also stronger fliers and rest with their wings held flat, whilst damselflies rest with theirs held together. In the air dragonflies are reminiscent of fast and acrobatic fighter planes while damselflies resemble slow but manoeuvrable helicopters.

In essence, this analogy with different flying machines is appropriate, as both families of insects have evolved to fill different econiches within shared habitats. Dragonflies are designed for the pursuit of larger and faster-flying prey, which may take them far away from water. Indeed, many species wander and migrate considerable distances in search of mates, good hunting and new places to breed and colonise. Damselflies, on the other hand, are not designed for long-haul flight. They tend to remain fairly close to water and they hunt smaller and slower-flying prey.

For both dragonflies and damselflies, the primary sense is sight. They have very large compound eyes, which provide them with sharp images of their surroundings and a heightened sense of movement that enables them to spot prey as it passes. To save on energy, they often use perches from which to fly sorties. When perched they can be seen to rotate and tilt their heads in order to keep a lookout for anything that moves, as it may be a suitable meal.

▼◢ The male common blue damselfly (*Enalagma cyathigerum*) and the male azure damselfly (*Coenagrion puella*) are difficult to separate in the field. The side of the thorax of the common blue has just one thin black band, while that of the azure also has an incomplete black streak. There is also a 'vertebra'-shaped black mark at the end of the azure's tail.

Dragonflies and damselflies are among the insects that develop by incomplete metamorphosis. They have nymphs, instead of larvae, which resemble the adult form and gradually increase in size. Their nymphs inhabit water and are also predatory, feeding on a range of invertebrates and small vertebrates. They are equipped with an extending lower jaw, which is used to grab prey in much the same way that a chameleon uses its tongue. Development can take two, three or four years, depending on the species and the availability of food. When fully grown the nymphs exit the water by climbing the stems of plants. The winged adult insects then emerge, leaving empty exoskeletons called exuviae.

As there are quite a few different British dragonflies and damselflies, most garden pools and ponds will be colonised by at least one species, as long as the water is permanent and is home to an ecosystem that will provide prey species. The remarkable thing is that new ponds are colonised by animals and plants very quickly without intervention, because water species have evolved to find their way to water. Those that cannot fly or walk manage to hitch rides on other organisms or float on the breeze, so that aquatic communities soon become established, with all the necessary biodiversity needed for a proper ecological system.

Of course, dragonfly and damselfly nymphs can fall prey to larger animals too, so they rely on camouflage to avoid being eaten. They are rather flat in profile and cryptically coloured, so that they are virtually invisible where they lurk in the mud and algae at the bottom.

Male dragonflies and damselflies transfer their sperm to a pouch beneath the base of the tail. This frees-up the end of the tail to clasp the neck of a female, which enables her to lay eggs underwater with the help of her mate. Before laying her eggs, the female curls her tail beneath the male to collect the sperm and fertilise the eggs. For a while the insects form a loop, as they are connected at two points. The females of some species will completely submerge in order to lay eggs deep enough to avoid them drying out in hot summers, so they rely on the males to pull them out of the water. Others have abandoned this strategy and simply drop their eggs on the surface of deeper water so that they sink to a suitable depth.

▲ The female common blue-tail damselfly (*Ischnura elegans*), like all female damselflies and dragonflies, curls her tail forwards to collect a sperm packet that the male has placed beneath his abdomen. The male clasps the female behind her neck so that he can help her lay her eggs when copulation is completed. Most insects mate tail to tail, or with the male mounting the female, but dragonflies and damselflies have had to evolve their own technique.

Dragonflies and damselflies are often adorned with beautiful iridescent colours, in greens, blues, reds, yellows, purples and oranges, making them rather impressive insects. The larger dragonflies are generally known as hawkers, while medium species are known as chasers and small species are known as darters. Larger damselflies are known as demoiselles, while smaller species are known as plain damsels. Although some species remind people of wasps and hornets, because of their striped colouring, dragonflies and damselflies cannot sting.

Photographing dragonflies and damselflies can be a rewarding and challenging pastime. As with butterflies and moths, the best results come with patience and learning how to approach the insects so that the macro-lens is only a matter of inches away. It is also important to position the camera so that most of the subject is within the field of focus, which can be quite shallow with macro-lenses. It is best to take a number of shots if possible, as one or two images will usually stand out against the rest in terms of focus, lighting, colour, pose and framing.

The hawker dragonflies are among the largest of Britain's insects, along with hawk moths, the stag beetle and the great green bush cricket. As such they hold a special place in the hearts of entomologists, young and old, professional and amateur. Large insects always impress because they stand out in contrast with those of more typical size. The sight of a hawker patrolling a garden can certainly be quite distracting and it is a good indication that the habitat has an abundance of prey.

▲▼ The large red damselfly (*Pyrrhosoma nymphula*) is far more common and widespread than the small red damselfly (*Ceriagrion tenellum*). It is also marginally larger and has black legs instead of red.

▼ The red-eyed damselfly (*Erythromma najas*) looks like a curious and pretty hybrid between blue and red damselfly species.

▲◀▲▼ The two demoiselle species are far larger than the other damselflies and look rather like butterflies when they are flying, as they flap their wings full and slowly. The females of the beautiful demoiselle (*Calopteryx virgo*) and the banded demoiselle (*C. splendens*) are very similar, but the males are distinguishable by their wings. Those of the beautiful demoiselle are uniformly tinted in blue, while those of the banded demoiselle have a broad blue band.

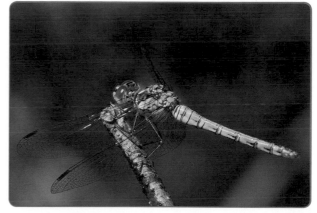

◀▲ The common darter (*Sympetrum striolatum*) is one of a number of small dragonflies. It is often found considerable distances from water and uses a favourite perch for flying hunting sorties.

◀▲ ▼▶ The black-tailed skimmer (*Orthetrum cancellatum*) and the broad-bodied chaser (*Libellula depressa*) are medium-sized dragonflies. Both the males and females have similar colouring between species, but the skimmer is far slimmer than the chaser.

▲ Although the golden-ringed dragonfly (*Cordulegaster boltoni*) has the black and yellow livery of wasps and hornets, it is not at all harmful. Mind you, all large dragonflies are quite capable of delivering a nip to the finger if they are captured.

▶ Aeshna dragonflies, such as the common hawker (*Aeshna juncea*), are typically seen patrolling hedgerows and forest margins in search of their prey, which comprises a wide variety of other flying insects.

◤ This dragonfly is called the emperor (*Anax imperator*) because it is Britain's largest species and the male is royal blue. The female is similar, but predominantly green rather than blue. The emperor dragonfly will eat other insects as large as wasps, butterflies and even smaller dragonflies and damselflies.

▼ The brown hawker (*Aeshna grandis*) is well named, as it looks as if its body and wings have been stained brown. This specimen had lost part of its forewing, but was still perfectly able to fly.

Insect watching

Appreciating British wildlife is often a matter of scale, as many of the most interesting species are among the invertebrates, which tend to be relatively small. Although they may be diminutive in size, invertebrates hold a certain fascination because they are innately alien to us in form and behaviour. That is to say, they are not based on the same body plan as amphibians, reptiles, birds and mammals, including humans. This lends invertebrates an unfamiliar quality, which arouses our curiosity. As a result we find invertebrates rather weird in comparison with vertebrates. Sometimes that weirdness translates into feelings of wariness and fear, but it usually translates into feelings of intrigue and attraction. We enjoy watching them going about their business in a miniaturised and different world to our own. The differences in scale and design mean that we live in parallel worlds, occupying the same space but one inside the other.

To invertebrates even a small garden is a vast wilderness, and the business of survival usually keeps them so preoccupied that they don't even notice when people take the time to observe

them. That is one of the advantages of studying invertebrates, as they are much easier to watch going about their lives than those animals higher up the evolutionary tree. They are often more visually striking than vertebrates too, which appeals to the natural human appreciation for colours, patterns and forms. We are somehow drawn to beauty in miniature, and British invertebrates include some of the most beautiful creatures one could hope to see anywhere in the world. If we only take the time to use our eyes properly then the rewards are often fulfilling and satisfying on many levels.

Although the world of invertebrates is described as 'micro' (meaning small) the term 'macro' (meaning large) is used when describing the technology used to observe and study invertebrates in the field, because it is used to magnify them so that we can see them in more intimate detail than we can with the naked eye. Magnifying glasses, eye lenses and camera lenses are all available for making macro examinations in this way.

Many invertebrates can be watched in their natural setting, but it is sometimes desirable to catch specimens for closer examination. A number of techniques can be employed for this purpose:

Tree shaking

By placing an old sheet beneath a tree or shrub, and then giving the branches a sharp tap with a stick, many invertebrates can be collected as they fall to the ground.

Pooter

The pooter is basically a miniature vacuum cylinder used to collect small invertebrates by sucking them up with a flexible tube so that they are unharmed.

Sweep net

This type of net is good for catching flying insects, as they can be held in the folded end of the sleeve until placed into a jar or cage.

Pitfall trap

Some invertebrates can be caught by setting a simple trap which they fall into but cannot climb out of. Bait can often be used to lure them in the first place.

Jars and cages

All manner of jars and cages can be used to house invertebrates while they are under scrutiny.

Macro lenses

A number of different macro lenses are available for making close-up observations of invertebrates. If it is necessary to go very small, then a microscope may be useful as well.

▲▶ The robber flies are so called because they appear to rob other insects of their food. In fact, they rob them of their lives, by catching the insects in mid-air and sucking out their body fluids. Both the hornet robber fly (*Asilus crabroniformis*) and grey robber fly (*Eutolmus rufibarbis*) species show the large proboscis for feeding and the low-slung legs to prevent injury from struggling prey.

Diptera – flies

Although many insects have wings and are often described as 'flies', true flies are distinguished by having a single pair of wings rather than two pairs. The second pair have been reduced, by the process of evolution, into tiny club-shaped balancing organs called halteres. This enables true flies to be very accomplished fliers, capable of precise aerial manoeuvring, acrobatics, hovering and even flying backwards. However, true flies have diversified greatly since the development of halteres, so that some are far more skilled in the air than others. The true flies include hoverflies, blowflies, horse flies, house flies, parasitic flies, robber flies, dung flies, bee flies, louse flies, mosquitoes, gnats, crane flies, midges and fruit flies.

The mouthparts of flies are designed for sucking fluids. Some have a piercing proboscis for reaching their liquid food by penetrating surfaces, such as the skin of vertebrates, the exoskeleton of invertebrates and the cuticles of plants. Others have a dabbing proboscis for lapping at liquids already on surfaces, such as juices on fruits, nectar in flowers and blood on carrion. Some flies can also dissolve dried foods on surfaces by adding spittle, which is then sucked up again.

The larvae of flies are also quite varied in the foods and econiches in which they live. Probably the most familiar are maggots, which live in rotting animal or plant matter, depending on the fly species. There are other fly larvae that live in still water, in soil, in rotten wood and in dung. Also, a number of fly larvae are predators, such as those of various

▼▶ Female horseflies feed on blood to provide nutrition for their eggs, while the males feed from flowers. The giant (*Tabanus sudeticus*) and the bronze-eye (*Chrysops relictus*) horseflies both have the large compound eyes typical of the family.

hover flies, which hunt aphids. Flies are an essential component of garden ecosystems, because they provide food for many other animals and play an important role in the decomposition and recycling of nutrients which, in turn, keeps the ground fertile and the habitat fecund.

The number of fly species recorded in a habitat is a good indicator of how valuable the habitat is in ecological terms. This is because fly larvae feed on a variety of food stuffs, so the more species then the more econiches there must be available within the habitat. For example, different fly larvae will feed on rotting fruit, animal dung, decaying wood, soil detritus, putrefying flesh, aphids, aquatic mud and so on. In turn, the flies are food to a variety of other animals, including spiders, bats and birds.

If you make a point of recording the fly species you see in your garden, then you will have a fairly good idea of how healthy it is as a habitat. Twenty species is a good number, thirty species is better, forty species is excellent and fifty species is outstanding. Of course, different flies emerge at different times of year, so it is best to record them over the whole summer, from April to September.

► This broad centurion soldier fly (*Chloromyia formosa*) is the male of the species. The female has a bluish abdomen rather than bronze.

▲ Two-tone hoverfly (*Xanthogramma pedissequum*), ribbed hoverfly (*Syrphus ribesi*), tiny tiger hoverfly (*Episyrphus balteatus*), bumble hoverfly (*Volucella bombylans*), drone fly (*Eristalis tenax*) and diaper fly (*Volucella pellucens*). Hoverflies were given their name because they are expert fliers, able to hover and even fly backwards when necessary. They use mimicry as a survival strategy, resembling wasps, hornets, bumblebees and honeybees, so that birds are disinclined to try catching them for fear of being stung.

▲ Like some hoverflies, the large bee fly (*Bombylius major*) is a bumblebee mimic. Unlike hoverflies, bee flies feed while hovering, in the manner of hummingbirds and some hawk moths.

▲▼ Crane fly larvae are the large maggots known as leatherjackets found in garden lawns, where they feed on plant roots. The adults emerge and reproduce without feeding. Varieties depicted here are the olive-grey cranefly (*Tipula oleracea*) and the large cranefly (*Tipula maxima*).

▲◣ The bottle flies are also known as blowflies, due to their larvae making rotten carcasses 'fly blown'. The green bottle (*Lucilia caesar*) and the blue bottle (*Calliphora vomitoria*) are both common or garden species.

▼ Like those of blowflies, the larvae of the flesh fly (*Sarcophaga carnaria*) also feed on putrefying meat. However, the flesh fly deposits young maggots, as the eggs hatch within the mother's body; this is called ovoviviparity.

▶ The common house mosquito (*Culex pipiens*) is widespread in the northern hemisphere, where it often finds its way into houses. Only the female feeds on blood to provide nutrition for her eggs. The larvae live in still freshwater, such as ponds, puddles and water butts.

▲◥▶ Grasshoppers vary a good deal in size and colouration, making different species tricky to identify with certainty in the field or garden. They feed on a number of grass species and are well camouflaged. Grasshopper varieties depicted here are the meadow (*Chorthippus parallelus*), common green (*Omncestus viridulus*) and field (*Chorthippus brunneus*).

Orthoptera – grasshoppers, groundhoppers and crickets

Grasshoppers, groundhoppers and crickets are insects of sward and undergrowth, so they need habitat with plenty of long grass and thicket. They all have characteristically large hind legs adapted for jumping, and most have wings as adults. This allows them to escape predators and to travel from one patch of habitat to another, in search of food and mates. Many are cryptically camouflaged, so that their colour and shape enables them to sit unseen by enemies.

Grasshoppers and groundhoppers are very compact in form when they hold their legs against the body, and they have very short antennae. This enables them to perch and move between blades of grass, from which they feed. They lay their eggs in the ground, so they like grassy places with areas of loose or sandy soil. While grasshoppers tend to be the colour of grasses – greens, yellows, beiges and even purples – groundhoppers tend to be patterned with blacks, greys and browns, so that they become almost impossible to locate when they sit on the ground.

Crickets are broadly divided into two families – true crickets and bush crickets. True crickets are terrestrial, or ground-living, insects. They have rounded heads and are adapted for living in shallow burrows, with relatively short legs and brownish colouring. Bush crickets are far more often seen in gardens as they clamber through undergrowth with their much longer legs and greenish colouring. Female bush crickets have scimitar-like ovipositors, which they use to insert their eggs into the stems of plants. All crickets have long antennae.

While grasshoppers and groundhoppers are herbivores, true crickets and bushcrickets are omnivores and will eat a wide variety of plant and animal matter. As these insects spend their time concealed by foliage, they communicate by making surprisingly loud calls, which betray their presence. Their calls are made by a process called stridulation. They do this by either rubbing their wings together or by rubbing a leg against a wing to generate vibrations. Different species produce calls with different notes and patterns. The sound of chirping crickets is synonymous with balmy summer nights across Britain.

▼ Groundhoppers are grasshoppers adapted to living on the ground, where they are camouflaged to look like pieces of detritus. The common groundhopper (*Tetrix undulate*) is very small and difficult to spot when it lands.

▲▼▼▶ Speckled bush cricket (*Leptophyes punctatissima*), oak bush cricket (*Meconema thalassinum*) and dark bush cricket (*Pholidoptera griseoaptera*). Female bush crickets are known for their scimitar-like ovipositors, which are sometimes mistaken for stings. They are used to split open the soft stems of plants, inside which the eggs are laid.

▼ The giant or great green bush cricket (*Tettigonia viridissima*) is an impressive insect. It favours scrubby habitat, with a good mix of tall grasses and ruderal plants on which to hunt for food.

▼ The wood cricket (*Nemobius sylvestris*) belongs to the family of true crickets, which have rounded heads for pushing their way through undergrowth and humus in search of food at ground level.

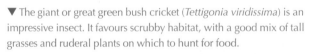

Miscellaneous insects

Most British insects belong to orders containing many species, but there are further insects that belong to orders with relatively few British species. Many are commonly seen in our gardens.

Earwigs

The name 'earwig' is a contraction of 'ear-wiggler'. The insects are often found in the seed heads, or ears, of corn and other grasses, and they have the habit of vigorously wiggling their bodies as a defence against predators. This name has led to the amusing idea that the insects are inclined to enter human ears. However, it may be true that harvesting medieval farmers occasionally experienced this, because disturbed earwigs will do their best to hide from predators by heading for the nearest dark recess.

Earwigs feed mainly on soft plant matter, but will also eat carrion. Female earwigs carefully tend their eggs and nurture their young with regurgitated food, which is behaviour usually seen in social insects. When food is scarce the female will sacrifice herself to provide nutrition for her nymphs. Male earwigs have an unusual breeding strategy, as they possess penises that detach within the females following insemination to prevent other males from mating. What is more, they have two penises so that they have a second chance at mating if the first attempt results in a breakage.

The forceps-like pincers on the tail are used for physical defence, for feeding and for grooming. Those of the male are curved, while those of the female are straighter. They cannot bite or sting, despite their habit of curling their pincers over the body when threatened. Earwigs are able to fly, but are seldom seen airborne. Their wings are double-

▼ Scorpion fly (*Panorpa communis*), snake fly (*Raphidia notata*), black caddis fly (*Sericostoma personatum*), alder fly (*Sialis lutaria*), brown lacewing (*Sisyra fuscata*), green lacewing (*Chrysops perla*), golden stonefly (*Isoperla grammatical*) and dancing mayfly (*Ephemera danica*). Scorpion flies, snake flies, caddis flies, alder flies, mayflies and lacewings are all primitive four-winged insects known from the ancient fossil record. They are not true flies, which have only two wings, and they tend to have rather weak and uncoordinated flight.

► Common earwig (*Forficula auricularia*) and tawny cockroach (*Ectobius pallidus*). Despite belonging to different insect orders, earwigs and cockroaches are superficially similar, being dorsally flattened and designed for creeping into crevices. They are also generally brown in colour with tough exoskeletons, and have omnivorous diets.

folded beneath short wing cases on the thorax to keep them clean when the insects forage within crevices on plants.

Silverfish, bristletails and springtails

These are primitive insects, found in humid soil and humus. They are abundant in suitable habitat, but rarely seen unless uncovered, because they are very susceptible to drying out. They live within microhabitats where there are predator and prey species that have evolved little since the dawn of terrestrial life, and all play their part in the nutrient cycle upon which larger organisms rely.

Lacewings, snake flies, scorpion flies and thrips

These are small to medium-sized insects with two pairs of heavily veined wings and weak flight. Many are predators of smaller invertebrates, such as aphids, which they hunt on the stems of plants within undergrowth. Thrips are very small with two pairs of fringed wings, and emerge in great numbers when conditions are warm and still. All have terrestrial larvae.

Caddis flies and mayflies

These four-winged flying insects all have aquatic larvae. Some species live in garden ponds, but they require well-established flora to ensure sufficient oxygenation of the water, as they breathe with gills.

Mayflies are famed for their short, or ephemeral, lives, which is why *Ephemera* is the genus name for the common mayfly – *Ephemera danica*. Mayflies emerge from the water en masse to outwit predators, which is why they have no need to live very long, as their sole objective is to mate and produce eggs.

There seems to be some confusion between mayflies and butterflies in popular culture, as butterflies are often

▼ There are many very small insects found in British gardens. They go largely unnoticed due to their diminutive size, although some species are conspicuous pests of plants, pets and people. Those depicted are silverfish (*Lepisma saccharina*), green springtail (*Sminthurus viridis*), flea (*Ctenocephalides canis*), white fly (*Trialeurodes vaporariorum*), bark louse (*Valenzuela flavidus*) and scale insect (*Coccus* sp).

mistakenly believed to live for just a day or two. However, butterflies need to live for some time to ensure that they manage to reproduce, because they don't emerge in such dense concentrations and therefore need to search for suitable mates. Depending on the species, the lifespan of butterflies ranges from between a couple of weeks, for those that live in colonies, to many months, for those that hibernate as adults.

Caddis flies are noted for their larvae, as they build protective cases in which to live. The larvae use pieces of gravel and plant matter to construct their cases to afford physical protection and act as a very effective form of camouflage.

Lice and fleas

Lice and fleas are wingless insects that parasitise other animals, especially birds and mammals. They are encountered in British gardens either on the skin of their hosts or in their nests. They feed on the blood of their hosts and infestations can cause infection and disease, as well as a general loss of condition. Humans can pick these pests up by handing infested animals, dead or alive, and by touching their nests, so care should be taken to avoid contamination.

Cockroaches

People tend to associate cockroaches with infestations in kitchens, where they scavenge human food and detritus. However, there are other species of cockroach that live in British gardens and have no interest in entering our homes, largely because they are adapted to the natural climate and therefore do not need to live alongside people. Cockroaches are omnivores that frequent leaf litter and rotten wood, where they find all manner of animal and plant matter on which to feed.

Multi-legged arthropods

Among the many types of arthropod are the millipedes and the centipedes, which are known collectively as myriapods, as they both have many legs. A similar, though unrelated, group is the woodlice, which can also be found commonly in British gardens.

Woodlice are land-living crustaceans, related to crabs, crayfish, shrimps and so on. They have many other local names, including pill bugs and armadillo bugs. However, these are misnomers, as real lice and bugs are actually types of insect. Woodlice feed on dead plant matter, including rotten wood. They can be found in moist, dark places, such as beneath logs and stones, where they find their food and remain hidden from predators. Birds will readily eat woodlice, so they only venture out from their hiding places under cover of darkness. Female woodlice keep their fertilised eggs in a pouch, so that they appear to give birth to live young.

There is a particular species of spider – *Dysdera crocata* – which has evolved to specialise in feeding on woodlice. As the prey is protected by armour plating from above, the spider needs to pierce the woodlouse from below, where its exoskeleton is much thinner. In order to do this the predator has enlarged fangs that are able to articulate to form a pair of pincers, so that one fang holds the woodlouse down while the other penetrates its underside. The woodlouse-eating spider can draw blood from a human finger, but its bite is not venomous.

Most woodlice are unable to roll themselves into a ball for defence, because they are adapted to squeeze into very small spaces, so they are quite flat in profile, rather than rounded. Those that can roll up are often confused with pill millipedes, because they look very similar and live in similar circumstances. This is an example of convergent evolution, as the two are not closely related but have evolved in a similar way because they have the same requirements. Woodlice have seven pairs of legs – one pair per segment – while pill millipedes have 18 pairs – two pairs per segment.

There are several types of millipede in Britain. As well as the pill millipedes with their domed shape, there are coiling or snake millipedes and flat-backed millipedes. They vary in design because they are adapted to different econiches and lifestyles. The name millipede means 'thousand feet', but this is obviously an exaggeration. British species have no more than about 100 pairs and usually far fewer, depending on the species. Like woodlice, millipedes feed on soft plant matter, and live in damp hiding places to avoid desiccation and predation. Woodlice, millipedes and centipedes all hatch

▼ Pale-edged woodlouse (*Oniscus asellus*), grey woodlouse (*Porcellio scaber*) and striped woodlouse (*Philoscia muscorum*). Despite appearances, woodlice are crustaceans and therefore more closely related to crabs and shrimps than millipedes and centipedes. They feed on decaying plant matter, including rotten wood.

from their eggs as miniature versions of the adults. They grow by moulting their old exoskeletons and expanding new ones, which are initially soft and pliable but then become hard and rigid.

The name centipede translates from the Latin as 'hundred feet'. Common British species range from 15 pairs of legs to around 35 pairs. Unlike woodlice and millipedes, centipedes are predatory hunters of small invertebrates. The larger species are fast moving and aggressive, with large mandibles for seizing prey, which they find beneath leaf litter, fallen timber, stones and so on. The smaller species are thread-like and able to penetrate the tinniest cracks in soil, where they specialise in preying on micro-animals.

▲ Here is a good example of convergent evolution in British gardens. The pill millipede (*Glomeris marginata*) and the pill woodlouse (*Armadillidium vulgare*) have evolved to look very similar because they live similar lifestyles, but they belong to different invertebrate groups. The woodlouse is a crustacean that once lived in water, like the freshwater shrimp, so the segments of its former tail have become compressed, whereas the millipede is a diplopod and has a single segment at the rear, because it never had a tail. They have both evolved to protect themselves from enemies by curling into a ball.

▲▶ Variegated centipede (*Lithobius variegates*), red centipede (*Lithobius forficatus*) and golden-thread centipede (*Haplophilus subterraneus*). Centipedes are hunters of small animals that live in the soil, leaf litter and humus, or under stones. They vary in size and shape because they are specialised at hunting in slightly different ways.

▶ Black coiling millipede (*Tachypodoiulus niger*) and red flat-backed millipede (*Oxidus gracilis*). Like woodlice, millipedes feed on decaying plant matter. Being long and thin means they can have large bodies yet still fit through small gaps beneath the detritus.

Molluscs

The most obvious species of mollusc in our gardens are the larger slugs and snails, but there are many smaller species that often go unnoticed, sometimes because they are mistaken for juveniles. Some are so small that

▲ **1–3** Pale-lipped banded snail (*Cepaea hortensis*), **4–6** dark-lipped banded snail (*Cepaea nemoralis*), **7** glass snail (*Oxychilus alliarius*), **8** plaited door snail (*Cochlodina laminate*), **9** amber snail (*Succinea putris*), **10** two-toothed door snail (*Clausilia bidentata*), **11** keeled snail (*Helicigonia lapicida*) and **12** garden snail (*Helix aspersa*). Snail species vary in size and shape quite considerably. This is because they are adapted to various ecological niches in our gardens. This means that they feed on different plants and live in different places, to avoid competition with one another. Garden snails (*Helix aspera*) used to be eaten as a delicacy in some parts of Britain and were known colloquially as 'wall shellfish' or simply 'wall fish'.

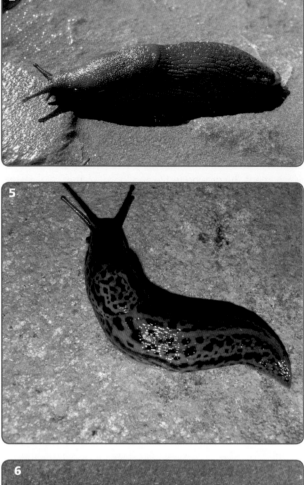

▲ **1 & 2** Red or brown slug (*Arion rufus*), **3** black slug (*Arion ater*), **4** yellow slug (*Limax flavus*), **5** leopard slug (*Limax maximus*) and **6** dusky slug (*Arion subfuscus*). Slugs are more catholic in their diet than snails, because they cannot afford to waste time being fussy as they have no shells to protect them as they forage. They can be found feeding on carrion, droppings, food scraps, pet food and algae, as well as the leaves of plants. Their slime is more viscous than that of snails, to help prevent desiccation, and they hide away in damp places until rainfall or dew makes it safe for them to venture outside.

they frequent the old tunnels of worms and remain beneath the leaf litter when they come out to feed.

Slugs and snails are generally vegetarian, preferring the soft new growth of herbaceous plants, but they will often eat a variety of other foods, such as semi-rotten plants, fungi, lichens, algae, carrion and faeces. As they have no shell, slugs are more reliant on moist hiding places to avoid desiccation, while snails are able to use their shells as protection from drying out. This means that slugs and snails can avoid direct competition for food by inhabiting different econiches within the same habitat.

Most animals are either the male or the female of their species, but slugs and snails are both male *and* female in one – they are hermaphrodites. They still need to mate with another animal of the same species, but it means

that they don't need to worry about finding individuals of the opposite sex. This is a useful survival strategy for creatures that move quite slowly and run the risk of drying out and dying if they need to travel too far to find suitable mates.

Snails of the *Helix* genus, including the garden snail (*H. aspersa*) and the apple snail (*H. pomatia*) have been eaten as delicacies by people for hundreds of years. In Britain their colloquial name is this regard is *wall fish*, alluding to their cousins the sea snails known, of course, as *shellfish*. In order to eat land snails it is necessary to purge them first. This involves feeding them on pleasant tasting foliage, such as lettuce, so that any unpleasant taste is removed. Large slugs are not so palatable, as they have tougher skin and a much more viscous slime than snails.

Worms

The most familiar worms seen in gardens are the earthworms, of which there are several similar species. Identification is further complicated by colour variations in species and differences in size due to age. In the adult form they vary in size from about a couple of centimetres (one inch) up to about 25cm (almost a foot), depending on the particular species. All of them live in damp soil with organic content, as that is their food. They consume humus along with soil, and the indigestible parts are excreted as a cast.

Earthworms play an important role in breaking down organic matter and aerating the substrate with their tunnels, which keeps the ground fertile and loose, so that new plants and fungi are able to take root. They are also a staple foodstuff of many animals, including badgers, moles and thrushes. In order to protect themselves from drying out and being eaten, earthworms are equipped with simple eyes along their bodies, which can detect light. They retract down their tunnels as soon as light is sensed, by flattening part of their body to act as an anchor by pushing against the sides.

▼ *Eisenia rosea* and *Lumbricus terrestris* earthworms. Earthworms play an important role in our gardens for various reasons. They help in the process of decomposition by digesting organic fragments mixed with soil, so that the nutrients are released for plants to feed on. They also aerate and drain the soil by making a network of tunnels. The same tunnels also act as passageways for other soil-living invertebrates, and they provide routes for the growth of plant roots and fungus mycelia. So the ecological community relies on worms for the physical infrastructure on which it is based.

There are other types of worm found in garden soil, called nematodes and white worms. They are generally very small, often just a few millimetres (a fraction of an inch) long, but can number in their millions when conditions are right for them. They too play an important role in breaking down decomposing plant and animal matter as part of the nutrient cycle. The presence of earthworms, nematodes and white worms is a good indicator that a garden habitat has the right foundation to support a healthy ecological community.

There are a few subterranean insect larvae that may be mistaken for worms. They include the grubs of chafer beetles and click beetles, the caterpillars of certain moths and the maggots of crane flies, which are often known as leatherjackets. On closer inspection it is usually quite obvious that they are not worms, even though they reside in the soil.

Leeches are aquatic and semi-aquatic worms found in ponds and damp places. Other freshwater worms include flatworms, sludge worms, roundworms, horsehair worms and segmented worms. In addition there are many aquatic fly larvae that resemble worms because they are legless.

Camouflage, mimicry and warning

The phenomena of camouflage, mimicry and warning colouration are found to one extent or another in most animal species throughout the world, including those in Britain. This is because animals are typically predator or prey species, sometimes both, so they use adapted appearance and behaviour to improve their chances of survival.

Camouflage, or crypsis, is the use of colours, patterns and forms to imitate habitat, so that an animal is difficult to detect provided it remains still and sits in the right place. Mimicry is a kind of camouflage whereby an animal imitates another species or sometimes an inanimate object in its habitat. In the first instance a predator is deterred from attacking because it thinks there is risk of injury. In the second the predator or prey fails to notice the presence of the animal.

Warning, or aposematic, colouration can be thought of as the opposite of camouflage, as a predator is meant to notice the animal's presence but leave it alone. It works because the predator learns to associate bright markings with animals that sting, bite or taste unpleasant. This is why some species mimic those with warning colouration, as predators cannot tell the difference and so leave both alone.

BEE BOX

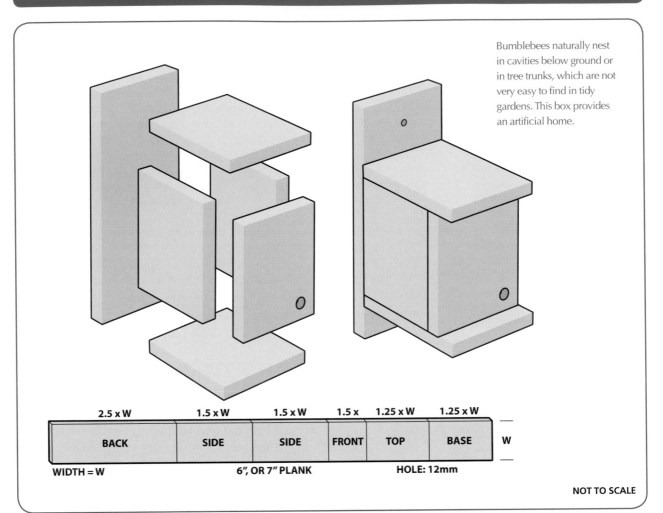

Bumblebees naturally nest in cavities below ground or in tree trunks, which are not very easy to find in tidy gardens. This box provides an artificial home.

2.5 x W	1.5 x W	1.5 x W	1.5 x	1.25 x W	1.25 x W	
BACK	SIDE	SIDE	FRONT	TOP	BASE	W

WIDTH = W   6", OR 7" PLANK   HOLE: 12mm

NOT TO SCALE

Kit:

This project requires only standard tools and a 6–7-inch plank of wood. The hole needs to be about 12mm (0.5-inch) in diameter.

Instructions:

1 Screw or nail the side panels to the back panel, making them level.

2 Fit the top and bottom panels.

3 Fix the front panel.

4 Add a covering of polythene or DPC with clout nails.

5 Drill fixing holes above and below the box.

6 Mount the box in a sheltered location.

BUG HIBERNATION BOX

Kit:

In addition to a basic tool kit, you will need a 5–6-inch plank and some lengths of bamboo cane.

Instructions:

1 Screw or nail the side panels to the back panel, keeping them level.
2 Fix the base and top panels in place.
3 Cut lengths of bamboo about an inch shorter than the depth of the box, and pack the void until it is filled – hammer in the last one or two to make everything tight.
4 Add some waterproofing polythene of DPC with clout nails.
5 Drill fixing holes above and below the box.
6 Mount the box in a sheltered location.

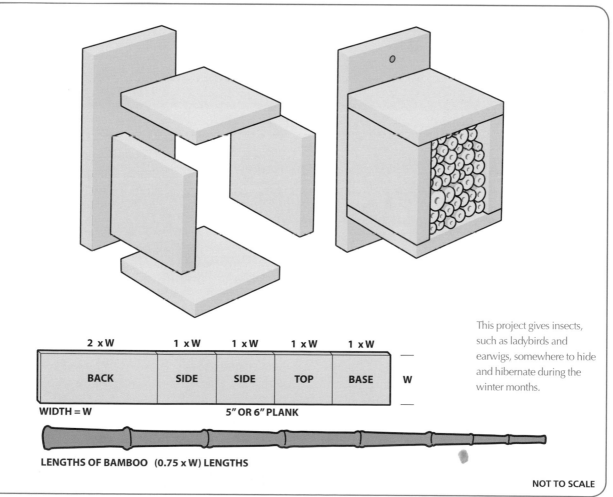

2 x W	1 x W	1 x W	1 x W	1 x W	
BACK	SIDE	SIDE	TOP	BASE	W

WIDTH = W 5" OR 6" PLANK

LENGTHS OF BAMBOO (0.75 x W) LENGTHS

This project gives insects, such as ladybirds and earwigs, somewhere to hide and hibernate during the winter months.

NOT TO SCALE

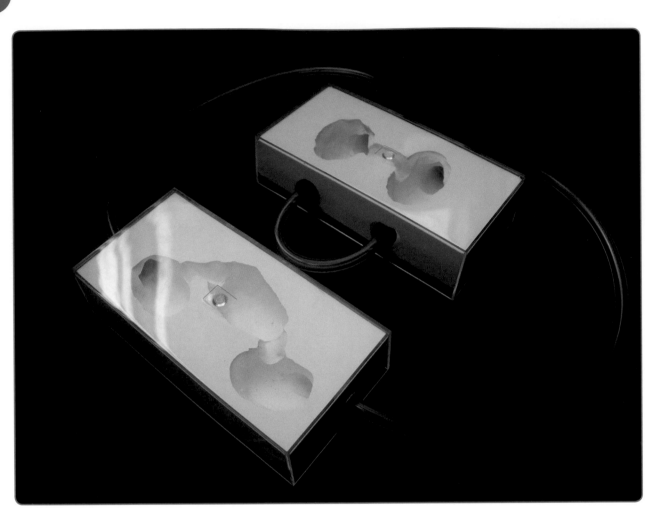

How to construct the formicarium's two key components – nest chamber and foraging chamber.

Formicarium

A formicarium is best described as a contained habitat in which ants can go about their lives inside and outside of the nest. The word 'formicarium' is derived from *Formica*, which is the Latin word for ant. As ants are so small it is possible to keep a population in captivity and study their behaviour as they go about the business of gathering food and nurturing their young. In fact, it is even possible to house two populations and investigate the way they compete and interact with each other.

The nice thing about making a formicarium is that it comprises different modules interlinked by the use of plastic tubes, which the ants happily travel along from one location to another. So nest chambers can be connected to habitat chambers in a variety of different ways, to see how the ants adapt their routines. It also makes life easier in terms of refreshing resources, as the ants can be locked out while maintenance is carried out.

Kit:

The transparent boxes are toy car display units, made from non-expanded polystyrene. They work well, because the gypsum (plaster of Paris) forms a close fit but also slides out easily. You will also need white modeling clay (Plasticine), polyvinyl tubing and rubber grommets (these are seals between the tubing and the display units).

Instructions:

1 Use the modeling clay to form the desired chambers and tunnels inside the display units.
2 Pour in the gypsum plaster and allow to set hard.
3 Remove the plaster casts from the display units and remove the modeling clay to leave the cavities.
4 When dry, replace the plaster casts in to the display units and mark where to drill the holes for the tubes.
5 Remove the casts and carefully drill the holes and fit the grommets.
6 Replace the plaster casts and insert the tubes.
7 You can have as many chamber modules as you like and you can link them up with the tubes as you see fit. If you want to lock the ants inside while doing maintenance, then simply fold the tubes and use clothes pegs as clamps.

FORMICARIUM

The idea is that you can study a colony of ants, using the chambers for different things, such as nesting, nursing and foraging.

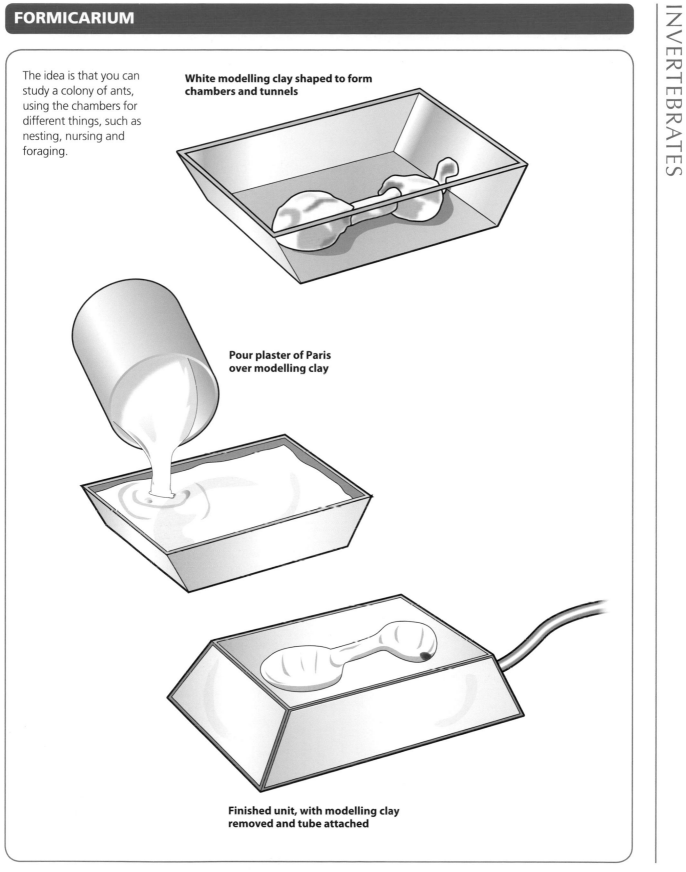

White modelling clay shaped to form chambers and tunnels

Pour plaster of Paris over modelling clay

Finished unit, with modelling clay removed and tube attached

AMPHIBIANS AND REPTILES

While people are generally aware that Britain has a number of species of amphibian and reptile, they tend to come across them relatively infrequently, because they are not conspicuous by nature. In fact they tend to shy away from observation, so that people usually only happen upon them by chance. This is largely because they would otherwise fall prey to predators, so it pays for them to be secretive and elusive.

Amphibians and reptiles are similar in various ways, because they are related, but they differ in one important respect: amphibians rely on water to keep moist and to breed, while reptiles have evolved to cope with dry conditions – they have scales over their bodies to avoid drying out and their eggs have leathery shells for the same reason. This enabled reptiles to properly colonise the land in prehistoric times.

Amphibians

It is fair to say that most ponds, whether large or small, will attract amphibians of one kind or another – newts, frogs or toads – to a British garden. As standing water is relatively scarce in the landscape in general, amphibians have evolved to become very good at finding it, because they cannot survive without it. For this reason new ponds become populated by amphibians quite naturally within a year or two, especially when they are surrounded by appropriate habitat and they are not compromised by the introduction of fish.

As adults, amphibians require habitat where they can avoid becoming desiccated, hide from predators and hunt for their invertebrate food. This needn't include a pool of water, but they cannot breed without it, so there comes a time when they have to find a suitable place for the purpose of reproduction. When ponds are unavailable, amphibians will sometimes resort to using any standing freshwater they can find, such as puddles in garden debris, but there is always the risk that the water will dry up before their larvae have had the chance to develop.

There are two common species of newt in Britain – the smooth newt and the palmate newt. They are rather similar in appearance. In fact the females can be difficult to tell apart, and the males are only distinguishable by looking at anatomical details that are more pronounced during the breeding season. The male palmate newt has webbed hind feet and a filament at the end of the tail, while the female has an absence of spots on the throat, which the female smooth newt usually possesses. The palmate newt is also rather smaller than the smooth newt, at approximately 70–80mm and 90–100mm respectively.

Unlike frogs and toads, newts lay their eggs singly and

▲ The smooth newt (*Lissotriton vulgaris*) is the only newt species found in Ireland. By sitting motionless at the side of a pond it is possible to observe the newts coming to the surface for air and then falling back or diving.

attach them to the foliage of water plants. A third species of newt, the great-crested, is locally common and may be found in gardens too, although it prefers larger ponds with shallow margins. This species is protected as it has suffered a decline due to habitat loss. It is larger again, at 130–150mm.

Frogs and toads belong to a different order of amphibians, the anurans. Unlike newts, the anurans have no tail and move with their bodies held above the ground. Frogs have greatly enlarged rear limbs, which enable them to leap considerable distances and to swim at great speed. Toads have smaller rear limbs and are more inclined to walk and climb, although they can jump if necessary. The

▼ The name of the palmate newt (*Lissotriton helveticus*) alludes to the hind feet of the male, which reassemble human palms in miniature. The filament at the end of the tail gives the impression of injury, but it is quite natural.

▼ Although protected by law, the great crested newt (*Triturus cristatus*) is locally common and often found in large garden ponds. It lives up to its name in the breeding season, when the male is adorned with large jagged dorsal crest.

▲ There is much variation in colour, pattern and size in the common frog (*Rana temporaria*), giving the impression that individuals belong to different species. It is a survival strategy, so that some specimens are always well camouflaged from predators.

▲ As the common toad (*Bufo bufo*) cannot easily escape predators it inflates its body and extends its limbs, so that it appears larger and more difficult to swallow. If this fails, then it squirts urine and secretes a noxious tasting substance from its skin.

common frog and the common toad are the most likely to be found in British gardens as both species are very adaptable and successful.

Both the common frog and the common toad vary a great deal in pattern and colour, including yellows, greens, browns and reds. The common frog has smooth and slippery skin, while the common toad is rougher and drier to the touch. This indicates that the frog requires generally damper conditions in which to live when away from water. The toad still requires moisture, but can tolerate generally drier conditions. This means that the two species occupy slightly different econiches and avoid competing over the same food resources.

When spawning the toad prefers shallower waters because it tangles strings of eggs around the stems of water plants. The frog, however, lays rafts of eggs, which float at the surface whether the water is shallow or deep. Ponds can become thickly populated with frogs and toads during the spawning period, but they soon vacate the water to leave their many tadpoles to develop. As only one tadpole needs to survive to adulthood during an amphibian's lifetime to maintain a stable population, it follows that the vast majority die in one way or another. It is a common survival strategy in nature for species to produce large numbers of offspring when they represent a food source for many other animals.

▼ The marsh frog (*Pelophylax ridibundus*) escaped from a pond in Kent in 1935 and has steadily spread across south-east England. It prefers large bodies of freshwater, but it does sometimes occur in garden ponds.

▼ The natterjack toad (*Epidalea calamita*) is not found in British gardens, as it requires special habitat. It is worth a mention, though, as it gets its name from the level of vocal noise, or nattering, from the male during spawning time.

Attracting amphibians and reptiles

In order to attract amphibians and reptiles to your garden you need to consider their habitat requirements in more detail than with birds and mammals. This is because they need certain conditions, as they are both cold-blooded and they have other characteristics that make them particular about where they are happy to live and breed.

Amphibians were the first vertebrates to move from water to land in the story of biological evolution. Although later vertebrates became entirely terrestrial, or land-living, the amphibians remained in an econiche still reliant on water. The adults can leave water, but their skin needs to be kept moist, and the eggs and larvae are aquatic. So amphibians need water and damp places in a garden.

Reptiles have scales, which enable them to avoid desiccation or drying out. This adaptation allowed them to become the first truly terrestrial vertebrates. In addition they evolved eggs with shells, so that they were no longer reliant on water. In fact, reptiles tend to inhabit warm and dry places, so that the typical habitats of amphibians and reptiles are quite different.

Nevertheless, it is perfectly possible to combine the habitat preferences of both amphibians and reptiles. Actually, this is desirable, as it makes for a better community of invertebrates as potential food sources. Also, grass snakes feed primarily on amphibians, so they do well with a mixed habitat.

The best way to create a suitable mixed habitat is to begin with a wildlife pond and then work away from it, so that there are areas of foliage, areas of open ground, areas of rockery and so on. That way, as well as having different microhabitats, the mosaic effect creates transitional areas too – perfect for amphibians and reptiles.

Corrugated iron

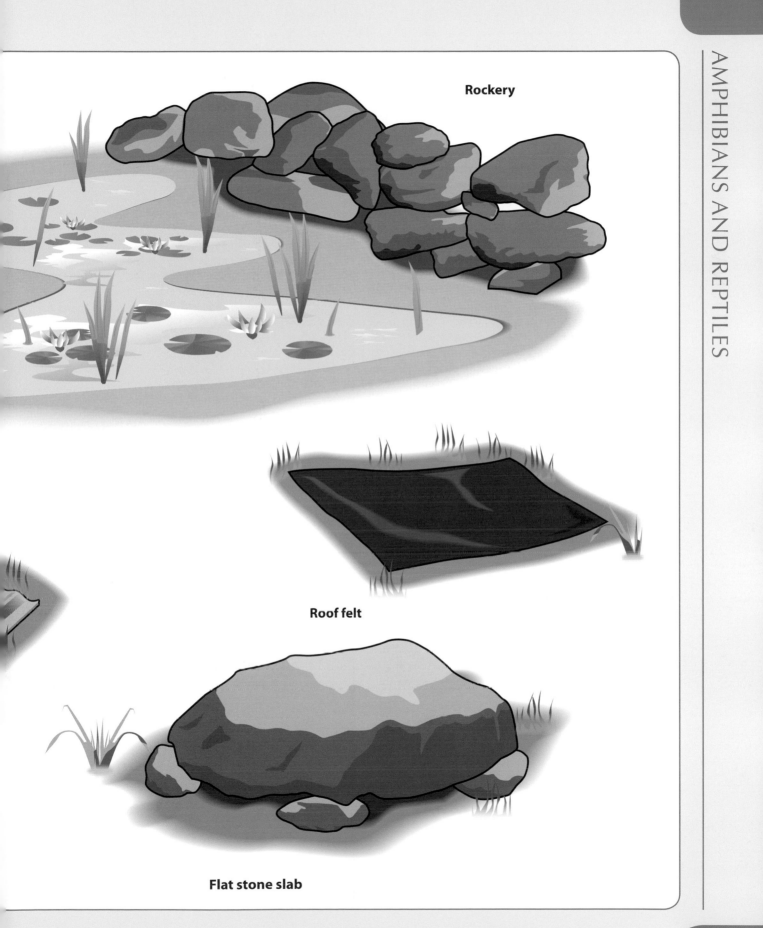

Rockery

Roof felt

Flat stone slab

Reptiles

In evolutionary terms the reptiles are more advanced than amphibians, as they were the first vertebrates to become truly land-living by losing their reliance on water, both to keep moist and to breed. They achieved this in two fundamental ways: by developing a shell for their eggs, and by developing scales on their bodies. This meant that reptiles were able to avoid desiccation, or drying out, and were therefore able to properly invade the land, well away from water.

Reptiles are still restricted, however, by remaining cold-blooded like amphibians. This is why a greater variety of both amphibian and reptile species live in warmer regions of the world. In Britain the reptiles are represented by lizards and snakes. There are two species of lizard likely to be found in gardens – the viviparous lizard (*Zootoca vivipara*) and the slow worm (*Anguis fragilis*) – and two species of snake likely to found in gardens – the grass snake (*Natrix natrix*) and the adder (*Vipera berus*).

Both of our lizards are unusual in their own way. The viviparous lizard is so called because it gives birth to live young. The eggs are retained in the female's body until they hatch, which means that the young have a better chance of survival. The slow worm is unusual because it has no legs, enabling it to tunnel into the humus layer. Both the viviparous lizard and the slow worm differ from snakes in having eyelids and in being capable of a phenomenon known as autotomy. This is where the tail detaches to distract attacking predators and then grows back. They also eat small invertebrates, as they are unable to dislocate their jaws to consume prey any larger than their open mouths.

Like the slow worm, both the grass snake and the adder lay eggs. The adder has a scattered distribution over Britain, and lives in south-facing, dry habitats, where it can optimise its exposure to solar radiation, which it needs to warm itself sufficiently for activity. The grass snake is rather more common, but is restricted to the more southerly regions and is attracted to watery habitats, where it preys on amphibians. Grass snakes will often take advantage of the warmth generated by rotting vegetation, such as compost heaps and grass clipping piles in gardens.

The adder is our only venomous reptile. It is reluctant to waste its venom on defence but can deliver a painful and potentially dangerous bite if provoked. The grass snake defends itself by vomiting and defecating if caught, which produces an extremely unpleasant odour. Most predators will be deterred by the prospect of receiving a toxic bite or having their mouth soiled with germ-filled faeces or vomit, so snakes are rather better defended than lizards.

Adders use their venom to quickly subdue prey in habitats where food is relatively hard to come by, so they need to be certain of a kill. Having bitten an animal, such as a small mammal, the snake will then follow it as it dies to avoid injury from claws and teeth. Grass snakes have no risk of injury from amphibians, so they simply grab prey in their mouths and hang on until the animal tires and then swallow it alive. Both species can dislocate their jaws to swallow large prey, which means that they can feed less frequently than lizards.

Our two other reptiles – the sand lizard (*Lacerta agilis*) and the smooth snake (*Coronella austriaca*) – are very localised in Britain because they are at the northernmost limit of their natural range and much of their shared habitat has been lost to development. They require warm, south-facing heathland. Like the viviparous lizard, the smooth snake gives birth to live young, while the sand lizard lays eggs.

Metal sheets

Our four common reptiles can be attracted to gardens by providing the right kind of habitat. They generally like patchy ground, with places to bask in the sunshine and places to hunt for prey. They also like places to conceal themselves

▼ The eggs of the viviparous lizard (*Zootoca vivipara*) are retained inside the female until they hatch and the young emerge, as if being born. The species should more accurately be called the ovoviviparous lizard.

▼ The slow worm (*Anguis fragilis*) can be quite numerous in British gardens. It feeds on soft-bodied invertebrates such as small slugs, worms and caterpillars, which it hunts at ground level among tall grasses and ruderal plants.

► As a defence against predators, the grass snake (*Natrix natrix*) defecates and vomits to produce a particularly unpleasant smell, while playing dead. The intention is to beguile the attacker into thinking the snake would be unsafe to eat.

when they are too sluggish to evade predators. In the wild this translates into crevices between or beneath pieces of rock or wood, where they can still warm themselves. For this reason, they are particularly attracted to sheets of galvanised iron or roofing felt left on the ground in gardens, because they can hide underneath while still increasing their body temperature considerably.

► The name of the adder (*Vipera berus*) is an evolution of the Middle English name *naddre*, which simply meant snake. Thus, 'a naddre' became 'an addre' and then 'an adder' over the passage of time.

▼ The female sand lizard (*Lacerta agilis*) uses warm, dry sand to incubate her eggs. As the sand is loose it is easy for her to bury the eggs and it is also easy for the hatchlings to disinter themselves.

▼ The smooth snake (*Coronella austriaca*) tends to be associated with heathland in Britain, because that is the habitat where it has been left undisturbed by human activity. However, it is also at home in areas of dry grassland and scrub.

Ponds

In many respects a pond is the ecological epicentre of a garden, so it is conspicuous by its absence. As well as the community of animals and plants that live in the water, other species are attracted by the opportunity to drink and bathe, as well as the opportunity to feed. In addition, the environs of a pond create a damp transitional habitat between the aquatic and terrestrial worlds. It is highly recommended, therefore, that a pond is installed in a garden if the intention is to attract a high diversity of wildlife.

Of course, a pond can be large, medium or small, so it is always possible to create a pond suitable for the garden in question. The only real proviso is that the volume of water is sufficient to prevent the pond from drying out, so that the inhabitants can avoid desiccation until the next rainfall or the next time we remember to top it up with the hose.

There are various ways to create a pond, but there are three basic types. There are rigid ponds, which use a preformed liner or a tank of some kind; there are soft ponds, which use a sheet rubber or plastic liner; and there are mineral ponds, which use clay or concrete liners. Of course, in some places the ground happens to be suitable to hold water anyway, either because the water table is sufficiently high or because there is an impermeable layer to prevent the water from soaking away.

Most ponds are set into the ground, so that wildlife can access and egress the water without difficulty. The first job, therefore, is to get digging. If a rigid liner is chosen then the hole obviously needs to be dug quite accurately to achieve a desirable fit, but a soft or mineral pond can be dug to any design as long as the chosen materials are sufficient in size or quantity.

Having dug the hole, in the case of a rigid liner it is best to back-fill any gaps with sand or sieved soil. In the case of a soft pond, it is best to pre-line the hole with sand and pieces of old carpet to prevent any stones from puncturing the liner when the weight of water pushes it in place. If a clay liner is used it is necessary to first line the hole with a mix of clay and sand. A second lining of clay is then applied using a process called puddling, which involves adding the clay in layers as the water rises, and kneading it to ensure a watertight seal.

If a concrete liner is used it is best done by adding a second lining of mortar to achieve a smoother finish, and by keeping everything damp to prevent cracks until the cement has cured. While the other types of pond can be used immediately, a concrete pond needs several months soaking for harmful minerals to leech out before plants and animals can be introduced.

To establish a wildlife pond community it is a good idea to add a bucket of mud, water and plants taken from another pond, a lake or a river, as it will contain many of the biotic components that form the desired ecological foundation. Purchased pond plants will also include other organisms, but most of the community will arrive in natural ways – on the wind, on the wing or by hitching a ride on other animals.

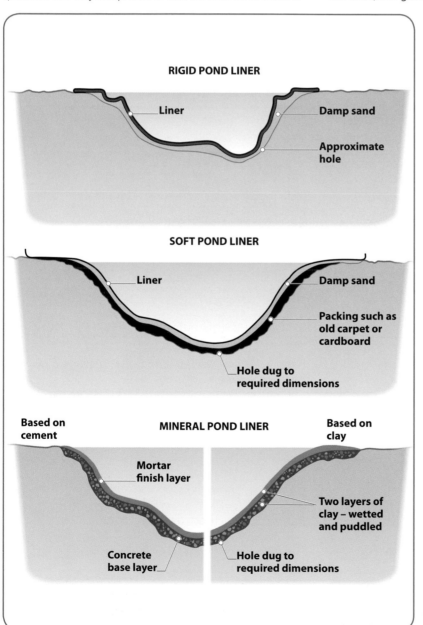

RIGID POND LINER
Liner
Damp sand
Approximate hole

SOFT POND LINER
Liner
Damp sand
Packing such as old carpet or cardboard
Hole dug to required dimensions

MINERAL POND LINER
Based on cement
Based on clay
Mortar finish layer
Concrete base layer
Two layers of clay – wetted and puddled
Hole dug to required dimensions

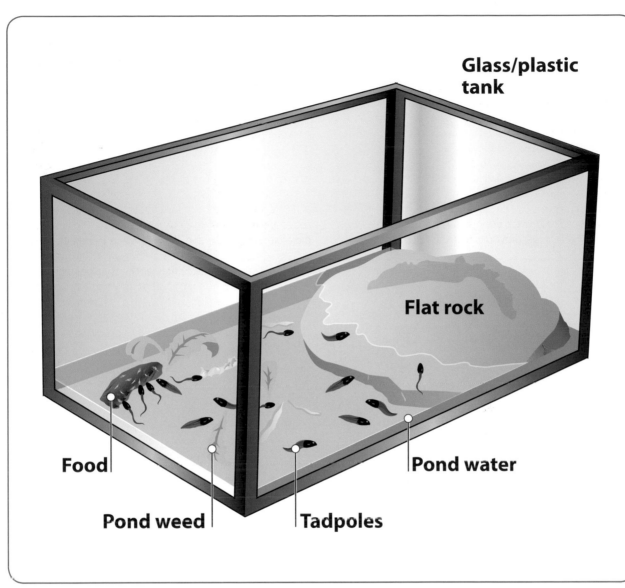

Glass/plastic tank

Flat rock

Food

Pond water

Pond weed

Tadpoles

Vivarium

Technically speaking any cage containing animals or plants is a vivarium, as the word transliterates from the Latin as 'place for life'. However, the term is usually used to mean a glazed container suitable for keeping reptiles or amphibians. The easiest way to make a vivarium is to simply use a fish tank or bowl, although it is also possible to use large sweet jars. They can be made from glass or transparent plastic, but the most important thing is that it is possible to reach inside with your hands.

For the sake of convenience and expense it is easier to keep amphibians than reptiles, as they don't require heat lamps and they eat foods that are easier to acquire. In addition, amphibians go through clear stages of development, making them more interesting to study. They are also easier to find in the first place, and rearing them in

captivity increases their chances of survival when released back into the wild.

In order to temporarily house amphibians for the purpose of studying them, the best thing to do is to collect their eggs or larvae from a local pond. They require shallow water and water weed, also taken from the pond, as well as a flat rock protruding from the water. This will eventually provide a means of leaving the water, but in the meantime it will provide a gradient on which the larvae – tadpoles – can rest at the surface. The tadpoles will happily feed on a small piece of unsalted bacon or a similar scrap of meat.

When the tadpoles have developed into miniature versions of the adult form they can be released into the habitat surrounding a pond, where they will find places to hide and ready themselves for hibernation in the autumn. There is little point in keeping them in captivity any longer, as the same process can easily be repeated the following springtime.

PLANTS AND FUNGI

British wild plants are essential for creating a British ecosystem in our gardens. So emphasis needs to be placed on removing introduced and cultivar species as far as possible if you wish to restore health and a true ecological balance to your garden, wherever it may be and whatever size it may be. This involves an adjustment of mindset, so that weeds are seen as welcome introductions, because they are simply the result of nature commencing recolonisation.

If we consider the character of a typical patch of British hedgerow or woodland, then that is the blueprint we should aim for. In other words an unkempt crowd of native species, competing for space and creating a three-dimensional habitat for both invertebrates and vertebrates to call home. This should include deadwood and humus, so that the process of nutrient decay and recycling is a part of the system. Try collecting wild seeds and scattering them in your garden, so that new species are added to the mix.

Plants

Ironically, many British people who consider themselves gardeners have surprisingly little general knowledge of, or connection with, our wildlife. Their interest in gardening is largely focused on the cultivation of showy and ornamental plants alongside manicured lawns. This means that wild animals are often considered to be unwelcome visitors and wild plants are generally regarded as weeds. In short, wildlife is their enemy, because this form of gardening is not really about embracing nature, but creating a picture of perfect artificiality. Of course, there is a paradox here, as the components they use are *real* plants. However, they are artificial in this context because they are either foreign species or they are cultivars, so they have no place in the natural environment.

In order to sway people away from this curious mindset and towards empathy with nature, it is necessary to educate them on matters of ecology. The aim is to elicit intellectual curiosity in natural history so that they see the point in creating appropriate habitat, and so that they develop a sense of responsibility as custodians of our wild fauna and flora. In most it will only be a matter of encouragement and guidance, but in some it will be nothing short of triggering an epiphany, because they have the misapprehension that gardens are somehow supposed to be unnaturally formal. Indeed, a few obsess about the tidiness of their gardens as if they are worried about what other people will think if any detail looks remotely unkempt and, dare it be said, *natural*.

The message then, is to allow our gardens to succumb to

the processes of nature to some extent, by realising that nature exerts its own equilibrium and structure to habitats, which is every bit as beautiful. It doesn't need to be all of your garden, but at least a part of it, where native plants are allowed to grow and provide the foundation for indigenous British habitat, complete with the insects and other animals that evolved here a long time before we humans began taming the wilderness and then divorcing ourselves from all

of the species that didn't fit in with our aesthetic plan. So, all of those who have the temerity to call themselves gardeners need also to be able to call themselves naturalists, so that they take pleasure in recognising the new species of plant and animals they manage to attract to their gardens with their new wildlife-friendly regime.

Plant species are grouped taxonomically just as animals are, according to their physical similarities and dissimilarities, because this is an indication of relatedness. Thus we have species, genus, family, order, class and phylum of plant or animal. Finally there are kingdoms to contain animals and plants. Fungi have their own kingdom too. As lichens are part-plant and part-fungus, so they technically belong to both kingdoms, but are classified as fungi for convenience.

Grasses

There are many types of grass native to Britain and the average lawn will contain a few common species. In the wild grass is grazed by many animals, which is why it has evolved to cope with being repeatedly cut back close to the ground. When grass has the change to grow into mature plants, it becomes more apparent that different species are present, because they have different appearances. They vary in height, in leaf design, in colour, in flower, in seed head and so on.

The many types of grass includes fescues, ryegrasses, meadow-grasses, cocksfoot, cockspur, bents, sweet-grasses, bromes, couches, wild oats, wild barleys, hair-grasses, soft-grasses, beard-grasses, reeds, catstails, foxtails, canary-grasses, feather-grasses, bristle-grasses and cord-grasses. Different habitats comprise different assemblages of

particular grass species, but they collectively form an important component of a habitat for a number of reasons. The leaves provide grazing for many animals, including grasshoppers, caterpillars and herbivores. The roots also provide food for various subterranean creatures, and the seeds are an important source of nutrition for birds and small mammals. In addition, the grass sward itself is an important habitat zone, where a biodiverse community of animals,

fungi and other plants live out their lives from the top of the grass stems down to the rootstock. Furthermore the grass serves to trap a layer of humus and condition the soil. Having a combination of short-cropped grass and mature grass in our gardens is beneficial, as it imitates the way that natural meadows would have margins of tall grass surrounding areas of grazing. The natural patchwork serves to provide habitat for further species that require something of the two.

Herbaceous flowering plants

Plants described as herbaceous are those that die back to ground level in winter and re-grow from rootstock or from seed in the springtime, as distinct from creepers, shrubs and trees, which develop woody stems or trunks from which to begin new growth. Herbaceous plants that last just one year are described as annuals, those that survive two years are biennials and those that live three of more years are perennials. In fact, grasses and ferns are herbaceous perennials, but here we discuss those plants that are often known as wild flowers.

Many wild flowers are ruderal plants, which means that they are the first to colonise bare ground, where they have little or no competition. These are the ones that are often described as weeds in British gardens, as they germinate in beds and borders or in the cracks in paving and walls and so on. In places where plant growth is already well established different herbaceous species are found growing, so that a succession of species makes up the natural plant community over time. This is why it is important to encourage floral rotation in our gardens if we want to

simulate a wild British habitat with a broad biodiversity of both plants and animals.

There are many families of herbaceous flowers. Some contain numerous species while others contain only a few. Together they contain a vast array of plants that inhabit the meadows, hedgerows and woodlands of Britain, which most gardens essentially imitate.

It is usually possible to identify the family to which a plant belongs by examining its characteristics, such as the shape and arrangement of the flowers and the leaves. For example, members of the daisy family are known as *composites*, because their flowers are actually many small flowers crammed together in composite form, which is why they have a large central hub. Other members of the family include thistles, dandelions, knapweeds, ragworts and marigolds.

Members of the pea or legume family produce pods of seeds, just like cultivated pea plants. This family includes vetches, clovers, wild lupins, vetchlings, trefoils and medics. These plants have nodules on their roots for trapping nitrogen from the air, which they need to grow. As a result they also fertilise the soil for other plants.

The carrot or umbellifer family includes parsleys, caraways, carrots, saxifrages, pignuts, ground elders, hogweeds, parsnips and fennels. They have parasol-shaped canopies of flowers called umbels, which provide a rich source of nectar and pollen for flying insects. The mint or labiate family includes bugles, germanders, mints, dead-nettles, sages, woundworts, basils, thymes and marjorams. The word 'labiate' means lipped, because the flowers of these plants look a bit like a pair of pursed lips.

Other herbaceous flower families include the carnation, buttercup, poppy, cabbage, rose, geranium, willowherb, primrose, bedstraw, nettle, borage, nightshade, orchid and many more besides. In some cases there are also a number of woody plant species within the family. For example, the rose family contains species ranging from herbaceous strawberries and cinquefoils to woody brambles, and raspberries and wild roses to plum, apple and cherry trees.

Woody flowering plants

In addition to the rose family there are many other flowering plant families with woody species, which are generally described as vines, creepers, climbers, shrubs, bushes and trees. Unlike herbaceous plants, each year's growth becomes woody, so that new growth needn't come from the ground, but from buds. They therefore form the semi-permanent structure of the undergrowth, hedgerow and forested parts of our gardens.

Small to medium-sized woody plants include heathers, gorses, brooms, brambles, currants, buckthorns, elder, spindle, privet, field maple, sallow, hazel, holly and honeysuckle. Many species form the under-storey of woodland, by exploiting clearings and margins, where they can compete for sunlight with the trees. The trees themselves belong to various families. These include the pine, willow, birch, beech, elm, maple, oak, yew and horse chestnut families. They grow into the mature trees that collectively form the canopy of British copses, dells and woods. Where they grow on forest margins, in small groups or alone, their foliage extends down to lower levels.

Flowerless plants

Before flowering and seed-producing plants evolved the world was populated by more primitive plants, without flowers and only able to produce spores. Many of these plants still live alongside flowering plants, as they are adapted to fill different econiches. They are the ferns, horsetails, mosses, algae, liverworts, lichens and fungi.

Seeds and spores both have their advantages and disadvantages. Seeds carry their own food supply, so that they can easily germinate and begin growing. However, flowering plants need to invest greater resources into producing seed, so they produce relatively few seeds and also need to work out ways of disseminating or spreading them to new areas. Spores carry no food supply, so they need to germinate in precise conditions, but they can be produced in vast numbers and they float in the air because they are extremely small, so they find themselves scattered far and wide without effort. In addition, as spores are microscopic in size they can lodge and begin growing in places where seeds cannot gain purchase, provided they have moisture and nutrition.

Many flowerless plants play an important role in the breakdown and recycling of nutrients in the environment. This is why they often grow on rotting wood and other organic detritus in gardens. In turn they provide food and micro-habitats for a diverse array of small animals of decomposition, which form the foundation for the ecological community as a whole.

For a garden habitat to be considered ecologically valuable it needs to comprise a healthy combination of both flowering

and flowerless plants, as that is what one would expect to see in nature. It follows that a rich floral diversity will support a rich faunal diversity, so that a complex ecological network exists, whereby all plant and animal species are connected and mutually dependent in one way or another.

For some naturalists plants are of relatively little interest, as they are merely seen as food and cover for animals. A botanist once said to a zoologist that he preferred studying plants because they don't move; the zoologist replied that that was exactly the same reason why he wasn't interested in plants. In fact, plants do move and exhibit behaviour, but it is in slow motion when compared with animals. Whatever one's preference, both plants and animals comprise the ecological community, so they should be accorded equal attention in our gardens if we expect a healthy microcosm of British wildlife to pass through or take up residence.

Fungi and lichens

Fungi are more primitive than plants and generally feed on decaying matter, so they perform an important role in the recycling of nutrients. The mushrooms and toadstools that we see are only the fruiting bodies of fungi, as their main component is an unseen tangle of fibres called the mycelium. Other, less conspicuous fungi include moulds, slimes and yeasts, which are also abundant in our gardens. The presence of fungi is a good indicator of ecosystem health, because it demonstrates the nutrient cycle in action.

Lichens are a curious combination of fungus and plant, known as symbiotic organisms. The fungus and the plant parts both provide something useful to the other, so they have evolved to live in union. The fungus provides the body, so that the organism can gather moisture and nutrients, while the plant provides photosynthesis, so that the organism has food. Lichens are able to colonise the most unlikely places, such as the surfaces of bark, timber, stone, bricks and roof tiles, where they often live alongside mosses and other primitive plants.

Out with the new, in with the old

Over recent years people have been encouraged to think of their garden as a kind of outside room, especially by garden designers. This has been bad news for wildlife because people have become unnecessarily precious about the appearance of their gardens, so that their plots have become overly tidy and well kempt, as if they care too much about what their neighbours might think. This unfortunate state of affairs has led to sterile and immaculate gardens that are essentially anti-natural, where wild plants are treated as weeds and wild animals are treated as uninvited vermin, for fear that the people next door might gossip behind the garden fence.

So this is a plea to all those seduced by such ridiculous and ludicrous notions: rid yourselves of your insecurities and find the chutzpah to shun the new convention and dare to keep a corner of your garden untidy, unkempt and overgrown. What has the world come to when a society is allowed to indulge in petty artifice at the expense of the natural environment from whence humanity evolved? There has to be something wrong when people have nothing better to do than obsess over bland conformity. Many people seem to have lost the ability to think for themselves and to appreciate the beauty to be found in the imperfection that comes with allowing nature and time to develop their 'golden stain', as John Ruskin famously phrased it.

Nettle beds

Although many people obsess about eradicating nettles from their gardens, in fact nettle beds provide valuable habitat for a diverse range of insects and other invertebrates. So a wildlife garden is incomplete without its patch of nettles. If you have the space you can always establish some nettles in a hidden corner of the garden alongside the compost heap and bonfire mound. As they sting and have nondescript flowers, it is understandable that nettles are unpopular relative to other wild flowers, but your garden will benefit greatly from their presence.

It is easy enough to contain a nettle patch, as the boundary growth can easily be cut back to prevent the plants from spreading. Of course, it is also possible to go to the length of inserting a subterranean barrier made from corrugated metal sheet so that the roots are unable to send out runners. Any seedlings that spring up elsewhere in the garden can easily be pulled out and disposed of. Gloves can be worn, but the plants don't sting if pinched at the base of the stem.

Perhaps the most desirable insects that require nettles are various species of butterfly, whose larvae feed on these plants. The peacock, red admiral, small tortoiseshell and comma butterflies are large and colourful species that grace any British garden and would be conspicuous by their absence. Their larvae can also be easily reared in captivity to study their development from caterpillar to chrysalis to butterfly. When released back into the garden they tend to stick around too, especially if there are suitable flowers for nectar-feeding and places for the adults to hibernate in the winter.

Nettle patch butterflies
Many people go out of their way to remove nettles from their gardens. This is partly because they sting as a defence against browsers, and partly because their flowers are not attractive, as they are wind pollinators. In addition they are invasive plants that tend to take over, so that large areas become dominated by a mass of uniform green. Despite their lack of appeal to humans, however, nettle patches support a considerable diversity of invertebrates, including four of Britain's most attractive butterfly species.

These four species are all members of the butterfly family known as Vanessids. They are the small tortoiseshell (*Aglias urticae*), the peacock (*Inachis io*), the red admiral (*Vanessa atalanta*) and the comma (*Polygonia c-album*). They are robust and strong-flying butterflies that hibernate as adults and are therefore capable of living for several months. They are also strikingly coloured on the upper wings, but cryptically patterned on the underwings to serve as camouflage when roosting.

The caterpillars of the small tortoiseshell and the peacock feed communally, while those of the red admiral and the comma feed alone. As they are all related the caterpillars are essentially similar in form, being covered in protective spines, but they vary in colour and markings between species. The caterpillar of the comma is the most interesting, as it has

patches of black and white which mimics the appearance of a bird dropping. When Vanessid caterpillars sense danger they immediately stop moving and will drop to the ground if they feel sufficiently threatened. When picked off a leaf they wiggle from side to side and exude a green fluid from their mouths, which is designed to impede the vision of predatory birds and give the larvae a chance of escape.

The butterflies are commonly seen in gardens because they feed voraciously on nectar to fuel their busy lifestyles and to accumulate energy reserves for hibernation and springtime emergence, when few flowers are available. They are particularly attracted to buddleia bushes, thistles and other large composites, because their flowers are robust enough to perch on and they produce copious amounts of nectar. Sometimes all four species can be seen feeding alongside one

another and in the company of an additional Vanessid species, the painted lady (*Vanessa cardui*), which migrates from southern climes but fails to survive the British winter. As its scientific name indicates, it is closely related to the red admiral, although its larvae feed on thistles rather than nettles.

Fallen and fermenting fruits are also sought after by Vanessids in the autumn, as their juices contain high sugar levels, ideal for energy storage. They often contain alcohol too, so that the satiated insects become languid and quite tame, making them easy to observe and photograph. They will often land on the observer while they are fluttering around in a state of inebriation. They can also be enticed to walk on to a hand, where they will use their proboscis to probe the skin for sweat to obtain the salts, which they naturally obtain by drinking from damp soil.

The chrysalises of Vanessids are often adorned with metallic markings, which seem to augment their camouflage by reflecting the surrounding environmental colours and otherwise make them look inedible to birds. Butterfly collectors were originally called *aurelians*, which is the Latin for chrysalis, and the word translates as 'golden ones' in allusion to this golden sheen which, in the case of the small tortoiseshell, can cover the entire chrysalis as if it were cast from precious metal.

Pest control

There are two ways of looking at pest control with regard to maintaining a wildlife garden. Firstly, there is the matter of using environmentally friendly approaches to controlling

plant diseases and pests, so that wanted plants and animals are not affected or harmed. Secondly, there is the matter of managing, controlling and deterring species that are undesirable in a wildlife garden for varying reasons.

In essence nothing can be genuinely described as a pest if it is a natural part of the ecosystem, but there is the matter of ecological balance or equilibrium, so that the wildlife garden contains a healthy biodiversity. Also, a wildlife garden is still a garden, rather than a patch of wilderness simply left to its own devices, so it is reasonable to want it to suit human use and appreciation too. We are not returning our gardens to the wild, but adapting them to accommodate wild species to one extent or another. It is a compromise between thinking of a garden as an extension to the home and has a connection with the natural world

Wild planting versus nectar planting

Although the aim of a wildlife garden is to establish a patch of British natural habitat, it is fair to say that some introduced plant species are useful for attracting and supporting populations of nectar-feeding insects, such as butterflies, moths, hoverflies, bees and flower beetles. These plants include buddleia, sedum, lavender and red valerian. Many have become naturalised in Britain anyway, because they have escaped from gardens and established themselves in wild environments. Thus they can often be seen growing alongside indigenous nectar-rich plants, including hemp agrimony, thistle, knapweed, cornflower and scabious. As a general rule these plants, alien or native, tend to have pinkish or purplish flowers. Other flowers that attract insects include yellow members of the daisy family, such as dandelion, and the umbellifers, such as ground elder.

The most important thing to remember is that 'variety is the spice of life' – that is to say, that the more species of plant in a habitat then the greater the variety of animals that will become part of the ecological community. So it is worthwhile importing wild plants into a garden. Seed can be collected or purchased for this purpose. Seedlings and potted wild plants can also be used, but note that it is illegal to dig up plants in the wild, and you risk arrest if you do so.

Incidentally, you should never pick wild flowers, as it prevents them from producing seed. It can also be illegal if they are growing on protected or council land.

The best way to maintain a diverse meadow is to raze everything to the ground in the autumn, once the seed has fallen to the soil. The cut material should be raked off and burned or composted, so that the soil is left virtually bare and low in nutrients. This prevents grasses from dominating by allowing ruderal plant seeds the light and space they need to germinate and grow vigorously in the following springtime.

Succession and rotation

It is important to understand that habitat left to its own devices will naturally undergo a process of change known as succession, because one generation of plant types is succeeded by another. If an area of land is dug over and left as bare soil, the first generation of plants to grow will be those known as primary or ruderal species. Their seeds may already be present in the soil, or they may arrive via the wind or be carried by animals in one way or another.

Ruderal species are not good at competing with other species, so they are eventually replaced by more vigorous secondary species as the ground becomes busier, so that there is more competition for light and nutrients. In turn the competition becomes vertical rather than horizontal, so that taller tertiary plants replace the secondary species. Ultimately woody plants replace the tertiary species because they have a head start when new growth begins in the springtime. This means that a bare patch of ground will eventually turn to woodland as the process of succession runs its course.

In most gardens there is insufficient space for areas of woodland to develop and undergo a natural rotation, whereby old trees fall to create clearings, so rotation needs to be artificially induced by managing the habitat as required. The best approach is to think of a garden as a patchwork of successive habitats, so that every couple of years an area is entirely denuded and cleared of plants and allowed to begin again. This is a simple way of imposing succession rotation, which roughly mimics the natural process and will ensure that the ecological potential of your wildlife garden is optimised.

More manuals of interest from Haynes

A guide to making environmentally friendly improvements to your home

Haynes

Eco-House Manual

Second Edition

Nigel Griffiths

ECO-RENOVATION • INSULATION • HEATING • WATER USE • MICRO-GENERATION

Haynes

Chicken Manual

The complete step-by-step guide to keeping chickens

Laurence Beeken

CIDER

Haynes

50BC onwards

Enthusiasts' Manual

The practical guide to growing apples and cidermaking

Bill Bradshaw

Haynes

Sewing Manual

The complete step-by-step guide to sewing skills

Laura Strutt

CHOOSING & USING A SEWING MACHINE • SEWING TECHNIQUES • TOOLS & EQUIPMENT • HOME FURNISHINGS • DRESSMAKING • PATCHWORKING • TROUBLESHOOTING

MEN'S PIE MANUAL

Haynes

The complete guide to making and baking the perfect pie

Andrew Webb

'Andrew Webb is a man after my own heart, and this book is packed with proper pies; go on, dig in!' Tom Kerridge

---

LAWNMOWER MANUAL

Haynes

A practical guide to choosing, using and maintaining a lawnmower

Brian Radam

Home-Grown Vegetable Manual

THE PRACTICAL GUIDE TO GROWING AND HARVESTING VEGETABLES IN YOUR GARDEN OR ALLOTMENT

Steve Ott

Haynes

Bee Manual

The complete step-by-step guide to keeping bees

Claire & Adrian Waring
Foreword by Bill Turnbull

Home Plumbing Manual

Haynes

THE COMPLETE STEP-BY-STEP GUIDE

Andy Blackwell

CENTRAL HEATING SYSTEMS • EMERGENCIES • LEAKS • BLOCKAGES • KITCHENS • BATHROOMS • PIPEWORK • TECHNIQUES • ALTERNATIVE FUELS • GREEN TECHNOLOGIES • EQUIPMENT